Contents

LONDON BOROUGH OF SUTTON

WALLINGTON LIBRARY | STORE |

This Book is due for return on the latest date stamped
below. When applying for renewal by post, telephone or
personal visit, please quote book number and date due for
return.

**Adults will be fined for overdue books. Children may
have their tickets suspended.**

27. AUG. 1968	11. OCT 75		
14. OCT. 1968			
	11. APR. 8		
21. OCT. 1968			
30. OCT. 1968	25. MAY 78		
	10. MAY 83		
27 NOV 1968			
-2. AUG. 1969			
11. JUL. 1970			
-8. AUG. 1970			
-5. SEP. 1970			
13. APR. 1971			
-4. MAR. 1972			
22. 10. 73			
26. 10. 73			

**If you cannot find the book you want,
PLEASE ASK THE STAFF.**

FRANK COUSINS : A STUDY

MARGARET STEWART

Frank Cousins: A Study

HUTCHINSON OF LONDON

HUTCHINSON & CO (*Publishers*) LTD
178–202 Great Portland Street, London W1

London Melbourne Sydney
Auckland Bombay Toronto
Johannesburg New York

★

First published 1968

© Margaret Stewart 1968

*This book has been set in Times, printed in Great Britain
on Antique Wove paper by Anchor Press, and
bound by Wm. Brendon, both of Tiptree, Essex*

09 087030 1

Illustrations

*The following acknowledgments are made for permission
to reproduce photographs: Frontispiece,* The Sun. *The
dockers (facing page 51), and headquarters (facing
page 66),* T.G.W.U. Record. *The house at Carshalton
Beeches (facing page 130), United Press International.
Blackpool TUC (facing page 131), P.A. Photos. All other
photographs, London Express Newspapers.*

Acknowledgments

The author's thanks are due to Sir Trevor Evans for his unfailing and generous help and to the *Daily Express* for permission to draw on their library; to Mr Jack Jones, assistant executive secretary of the Transport and General Workers' Union, for his invaluable guidance; to the TUC for permission to use their library; to the BBC for help in research in connection with Frank Cousins' broadcasts; to the Gallup Poll for letting me look at their records.

Thanks, above all, to the very many people in the Labour and trade union movement, in Whitehall and in Fleet Street, who gave so generously of their time and patiently answered my questions.

A special thanks to Hugh Chevins for having cast his critical eye over the MS and making many helpful suggestions.

To all of these I owe a great debt, but the responsibility for everything in this book is entirely my own.

Introduction

Frank Cousins has dominated the trade union scene since 1956, when he became leader of Britain's biggest union. As General Secretary of the Transport and General Workers' Union, with its massive block vote at trade union and Labour party conferences, and nearly 1½ million members scattered throughout the national economy, he has occupied a central position of power in British life. The subject of endless controversy and speculation, he has been at the storm-centre of politics, and never more than during the conflicts over nuclear disarmament in the late 1950s and over wages policy in the mid-1960s.

To many people he *is* the TUC. Asked to name a prominent trade union leader by a Gallup Poll in the late summer of 1966, 42 per cent named Cousins, compared with 29 per cent for George Woodcock. (A similar question put in 1959 produced 65 per cent for Cousins, while Arthur Deakin came second with 16 per cent, though he had been dead for four years!) Cousins symbolises to the public what is both good and bad about the trade unions.

To many he is the big union 'boss', one of the 'feudal barons' of modern society. To others he is the champion of the workers' rights, the fighter for the underprivileged. Most people find Cousins an enigma. I must confess that, even after writing this book, I still do myself. But he has been singularly consistent in his views on wages and industry, and it might not be too far-fetched to describe him as an enigma without variations.

I have known Cousins well since he first came to the fore and have followed his career closely, initially as the industrial correspondent of the *News Chronicle* and later, possibly with more detachment, from the outside. I have always been intrigued by his personality and his influence, and had in mind that one day I would like to write a book about him.

This is not, in any sense, a biography, official or unofficial. It is, rather, an attempt to study various aspects of his leadership and to set out some of the most significant events and episodes in his career. I have, inevitably, had to pound the well-trodden path from Brighton to Blackpool, and follow the annual conference merry-go-round of the Labour movement (Brighton, 1967, was my twenty-fifth TUC!). To some readers the business of resolutions, amendments, card votes and speech-making may seem tiresome, but these conferences have produced the decisive points in Cousins' life. They are the essence of his being.

Cousins' own life-story will be told when he writes his memoirs and for a full account of the agonising conflict over the prices and incomes policy we will have to wait the statutory thirty years for Cabinet papers to be released. But I do not see why one should wait until a public figure has left the centre of the stage before attempting to study him, or to assess his influence.

One of the biggest difficulties in writing about contemporary events is to choose a stopping- as well as a starting-point. This book begins, to all intents and purposes, with Arthur Deakin's death in May 1955. It could end on July 3rd, 1966, when Cousins handed in his resignation as Minister of Technology, or on October 5th, when the Labour party conference accepted the Government's incomes policy and rejected that of Cousins. This was the day which Cousins called 'tragic for our principles' and Ray Gunter, the Minister of Labour, described as a 'watershed'. We are not yet out of that watershed. November 5th, the date when Cousins announced his intention of resigning as a Member of Parliament, would be a tempting choice, or December 5th, when he did resign. January 1st, 1967, which saw the end of the deep freeze and the beginning of 'severe restraint', would be another possibility; or March 2nd, the day when the executive leaders of the trade unions decided to pursue their own voluntary incomes policy and firmly told the Government to keep out of collective bargaining. The decision of March 2nd, which was supported by Cousins and his union, marked a new stage in the ninety-nine years of TUC history and represented a move, however tentative, towards vesting centralised authority in the TUC General Council.

In the event, this book runs on until September 5th, 1967. This was the day when the full Trades Union Congress unanimously accepted Cousins' aim of a £15-a-week national minimum wage, reaffirmed their faith in free collective bargaining and decisively rejected the Government's deflationary policies. At this moment of time it seemed that Cousins' long, and sometimes lonely, stand on wages had been vindicated.

I have not, however, attempted to crystal-gaze into the future or to make any predictions about the success or failure of the TUC's voluntary efforts and their possible effects on the Labour Government and its economic policies.

Events since this book went to press (briefly dealt with in Chapter 17) have not caused me to revise any of my assessments. If anything, they have reinforced the enigmatic and unpredictable aspects of Frank Cousins' character. Though his policy on wages has been consistent, his course of action has often been shrouded in mystery. As in 1956, 'What will he do now?' was a burning question in early 1968, when a head-on collision over the prices and incomes policy appeared to be inevitable.

The material for this study has been drawn from Cousins' own speeches and statements, and from the records of the

TGWU, the TUC and the Labour party. I have delved into newspaper reports and drawn on my own recollections, diaries and articles, and talked to countless people who have known him at various stages in his career. I met both friendly and hostile witnesses, and one extraordinary feature to emerge has been the discrepancy between people's observations and assessments. Thus, two Cabinet Ministers gave me diametrically opposite accounts of what Cousins was like in the Cabinet.

Frank Cousins knew that I was writing a book, but I have not involved him in it, nor was I able to obtain his direct personal co-operation. I have tried to be objective and I trust this book will not upset the friendly relations which I have always had with him and his wife.

Three main questions have emerged during the course of my research. I do not pretend to have found all the answers, but the points they raise represent the key to an understanding of the subject:

1. How is it that the Transport and General Workers' Union, so consistently on the right in Arthur Deakin's day, swung so completely to the left under Cousins?

2. What has been the net effect of Cousins' consistent and persistent campaign against wage restraint on the prices and incomes policy?

3. Is Cousins big in his own right, or merely by virtue of his $1\frac{1}{2}$ million members and his union's block vote? Would he wield any influence, or be listened to, if he were the leader of a smaller union?

1

The making of a General Secretary

ON Sunday afternoon, May 1st, 1955, Arthur Deakin, the General Secretary of the Transport and General Workers' Union, collapsed at a May Day Rally he was addressing in Leicester Corn Exchange, and died a few hours later in hospital. Officials telephoned the news to Frank Cousins, who was at his home in Epsom with his wife Nance and their small daughter Frances. The Cousinses kept their phone in the front hall, and Frank left the sitting-room to answer it. A few minutes later he burst into the room: 'Deakin's dead,' he announced. This was to make an indelible impression on the four-year-old Frances. A few years later I was having supper with Frank and Nance and we were having a talk over a drink before our meal. Frances was playing with her jigsaw puzzle and I thought I heard her murmur softly to herself, 'Deakin's dead . . . Deakin's dead.' When she had been put to bed I asked Nance whether I had heard aright. 'Oh yes,' she said. 'Frances often says that when she hears grown-ups talking about politics.'

Arthur Deakin, who had been General Secretary of the Transport and General Workers' Union since 1945, actually had only a few months to go before he was officially due to retire, but his sudden death precipitated matters. It brought to an abrupt end an epoch in the Labour movement, when a small group of right-wing union leaders, wielding nearly half the total votes at a party conference, could virtually dictate Labour policy and ride roughshod over any opposition. This situation had caused Barbara Castle to cry out in anguish at the party conference in 1953: 'The Labour movement is in danger of dying a death of three million cuts—the block votes of four men!'

The four men she was referring to were Deakin, the driving-force in the alliance against the left, Sir William Lawther, the miners' President, Sir Lincoln Evans, the steel workers' leader, and Sir Thomas Williamson, General Secretary of the National Union of General and Municipal Workers. They formed a powerful consortium, dedicated to the pursuit of anti-Communism, anti-Bevanism and the smashing of any heresies which conflicted with their view of 'responsibility' in the Labour movement. They had used their combined votes to back right-wing policies, for example on German rearmament, and had usually acted in concert to elect only those who were politically 'reliable' to positions of influence. Industrially they had supported the Cripps policy of wage restraint and used their combined influence to further policies of moderation and oppose the use of the strike weapon.

Lawther, who retired in the spring of 1954, was succeeded by the Yorkshire Miners' President, Ernest Jones, a man of great sincerity but lacking the forcefulness and subtlety of his predecessor. Will Lawther, who silenced hecklers at the Morecambe party conference in 1952 by telling them 'shut your gob', was a canny Geordie; one of the best-read men in the movement, he nevertheless had a profound contempt for intellectuals. Tom Williamson, very much the junior member of the trio, was altogether too gentle and unassuming to be an effective hammer of the left. Lincoln Evans had left to join the Steel Board in 1953.

The question of the immediate succession to Deakin was already settled. A. E. ('Jock') Tiffin, a genial but not particularly effective London busman and the Union's Assistant General Secretary, had been elected General Secretary to take over when Deakin retired. Tiffin had served for some years on the Labour Party National Executive Committee and, although publicly identified with the Deakin 'hatchet-men' during the interminable rows over the Bevanites which racked the Labour party in the early 1950s, there was some evidence that he was, at heart, a man of tolerance.

'There's been too much blood-letting already,' he told me when I asked whether he would back the proposal to expel Nye Bevan for defying the Party Whip in the spring of 1955. On the fateful day, March 23rd, he cast his vote, along with twelve others, in favour of expulsion, having been successfully talked round. 'Jock was wobbling, but we managed to fix him,' a right-wing trade unionist confided to me on the eve of the National Executive meeting. All to no purpose, as it turned out. The executioners were outvoted by fourteen votes to thirteen and Bevan was reprieved.

Tiffin did not live long enough to show what kind of a union leader he would have made. Already a sick man, he died just after Christmas, 1955, having spent much of his term of office in hospital. Frank Cousins succeeded him as General Secretary in the spring of 1956.

It was thus owing to the accident of two deaths in rapid succession that Cousins, hitherto a relatively unknown union official, rocketed to the very top seat of power. With its $1\frac{1}{4}$ million members scattered throughout Britain, including some of the most strategic sections of the national economy, and with the biggest single block vote of any union in the Labour movement, the man who became General Secretary of this Leviathan could well be said to have reached the 'commanding heights' in both the industrial and political sense.

There were no signs in his early career that Cousins would later reach the top. He merits a mere footnote in Alan Bullock's *Life of Bevin*, and does not appear at all in a study of Arthur Deakin by V. L. Allen. One can search in vain through the voluminous press cuttings about him for more

B

than a bare mention of his name before 1955. We first glimpse him in 1945, when he became a member of a council for coal distribution, along with George Brown, very much his junior, who was then organising transport workers in the London area. Two years later he was appointed to a Government committee on petrol stations.

Apart from these references, he was reported as making speeches against the Conservative Government's plans to de-nationalise road transport in the early 1950s and was mentioned in connection with a few unofficial strikes in his own section. But he attracted no more national attention than any other officer of Deakin's union. Those who knew him and worked with him in the early days—among them George Brown—have spoken highly of his competence and capability as a union officer, and of his single-minded devotion to his job, but nobody, unless they were wise after the event, has claimed to detect the spark of future leadership.

Cousins, like so many of the older generation of trade unionists, came up the hard way. If the playing fields of Eton are the traditional training-ground for Conservative statesmen, the asphalt playgrounds of the elementary school have been the nursery slopes for most Labour leaders. Times have changed and nowadays, among the post-war generation, one finds many with a grammar school and university education. One of Cousins' own sons, Michael, went to Cambridge. But 'I left school at fourteen' is still the opening gambit of the life-story of many trade union leaders.

Frank Cousins, the eldest boy among ten children, was born in Minerva Street, Bulwell, on the outskirts of Nottingham, on September 8th, 1904. His father, a railwayman, moved to Doncaster to find work in the pits, and it was in the neighbouring colliery of Brodsworth Main that Cousins started work as a lamp-boy at the age of fourteen, when he left King Edward School. His father did not want him to stay in mining, and in 1924 he took a job with a coal dealer, driving miners' concessionary coal round the South York-shire coalfield. A few years later he moved to long-distance lorry driving, conveying great cargoes of meat and heavy crates between Yorkshire, Scotland and the South. On chang-ing jobs, he left the Yorkshire Miners' Union and joined the Transport Union.

His father had drummed trade unionism into him from the start and much later, interviewed by John Freeman on 'Face to Face' (BBC Television, October 1961), he recalled:

> The very first week I had a pay packet my dad made me open my first pay packet and join the Union with it. I thought he was a shocker—I wanted to take it home to Mum. But Dad said quite clearly, 'This is the place where you get your protection. You go and join the Union.' And that was that.

Cousins took part in the miners' strikes of 1920 and 1921, and during the General Strike of 1926 he drove a lorry for the Doncaster strike committee, collecting fish and bread for the strikers' kitchens. Many miles further south, another young man who was to play an equally crucial part in the Labour movement, Hugh Gaitskell, then an undergraduate at New College, was driving a bull-nosed Morris between London and Oxford, carrying supplies of the official strike paper *The British Worker* and other propaganda material. It was Gaitskell's baptism in a movement into which Cousins had been born.

In 1930, when he was twenty-six, Cousins married Nance Judd, daughter of Percy Judd, a railway clerk who had been victimised in the General Strike. The Judds were very left-wing, and Percy, who later became a Doncaster Alderman, ran a 'Bomb' (left-wing book) shop. Their home was the rendezvous for visiting members of the Independent Labour Party and other leftists.

A young and impressionable man like Cousins was inevit-ably caught up in the emotional wave of hatred for Capitalism which swept Britain at the time of the great depression. From his driver's cab, as he travelled the length and breadth of the country, he saw at first-hand much of the misery and tragedy caused by mass unemployment in the early 1930s. On the same 'Face to Face' TV programme he related an incident which had impressed him as a young man and confirmed him in his determination to fight against social injustice.

The story has often been told, but I think it is worth re-telling it here in his own words:

> I happened to be in a transport café on the Great North Road when a young couple came in there with a child in a nearly broken-down pram, and they were walking from there to London because the man understood he could get a job in London. And they came into the café and sat down, and they fetched a baby's feeding bottle out, and it had water in it. They fed the baby with water and then lifted the kiddy's dress up—and it had a newspaper nappy on. They took this off and sort of wiped the baby's bottom with the nappy they'd taken off and then picked up another newspaper and put that on for another nappy. I think if I ever felt a resentment against the system it was on that occasion. I thought somebody ought to do something about it. We had got through the disputes and strikes in 1926, but here was the oppression being brought home to an innocent defenceless child. It made a profound impression on me and I think it was one of the things I would regard as a highlight.

Lorry drivers were then one of the weakest links in the TGWU organisation. The employers were for the most part small firms (there were 3,000 of them in London alone) and managed to exist by undercutting each other and by exploiting their workers. It was an uphill job to negotiate proper wages and conditions for the men, who were themselves difficult to organise. A long-distance lorry driver is very much out on his own, driving all through the night, his only contact with the outside world being the people he meets in the roadside cafés or at the boarding-house where he sleeps between turns. It was not surprising that in the pre-war atmosphere drivers were often willing to put in longer hours for a few extra shillings, only too conscious that there were thousands of men ready to take their jobs if they did not comply with the boss's wishes.

Legislation was first introduced in the 1930s to regulate the conditions in road haulage. The Road Traffic Acts laid down safety standards, restricting hours and limiting loads, and established a licensing system. This legislation gave an impetus to organisation on both sides of the industry, and was undoubtedly one of the major achievements of Ernest Bevin, then General Secretary of the Transport Union. His efforts culminated in the Road Haulage Act of 1938, which established central wages machinery.

Cousins was an able and enthusiastic lieutenant in Ernest Bevin's campaign to recruit road transport workers into the Union, first as a voluntary organiser and after 1938 on a full-time basis. The story is told that Bevin spotted him at a union conference in Leeds, when Cousins had the temerity to challenge some of the General Secretary's arguments. Bevin, momentarily taken aback, was impressed and called Cousins up to him after the meeting. 'You'll go far, young man,' he said.

Cousins decided to make a really thorough job, and set out to be one of the best organisers not only of his own but of any union. Bill Goulding, then a branch secretary in South Yorkshire, has spoken of his untiring activity (*Sunday Times*, October 2nd, 1966). 'By God, he worked,' said Goulding. 'That's one of the things that really lifted him up. . . . He's done more for the lorry driver than anyone in England.' In a curiously revealing observation Goulding remarked: 'I know chaps that's driven with him when he was a lorry driver for Faircloughs. Off twelve fourteen-ton loads of meat he'd never as much as pinch a steak.'

Cousins applied for the post of national officer in 1944 and was subjected to a stiff and searching oral examination by a committee under Harold Clay (then acting Assistant General Secretary and a leading expert on road transport). Cousins stood up to Clay's bowling and impressed the examining committee with his knowledge of the road transport Acts and his grasp of industrial relations. His mentor at that time was Jack Corrin, National Secretary of the road transport group, whom he succeeded in 1948.

When Bevin became Minister of Labour in 1940 Arthur Deakin was appointed Acting General Secretary and was elected as full General Secretary in 1945. His relations with Cousins were outwardly correct, but the two men were mutually antipathetic. Deakin suspected Cousins' left-wing views and regarded him as the leader of a group of potential rebels. Some of the senior union officials resented the way in which Cousins so often acted independently and without consulting them; sometimes he even went direct to the employers to work out a settlement when there was a dispute. At least three times he was 'reported' to Deakin, and once pleaded 'inexperience' in his own defence.

As a union officer, Cousins kept his political views to himself, but his reputation for militancy in his Doncaster days had alarmed the hierarchy in London. Deakin, who was preparing to introduce a ban on Communists, carried out his own private witch-hunt and anybody who was not of his particular brand of thought was immediately suspect. Cousins, who was never in his life a Communist, refused to co-operate with such a McCarthy-type inquisition.

The conflict between the two men reached a peak in January 1947, during an unofficial strike of lorry drivers. A stormy meeting was held at the Memorial Hall, Farringdon Street, in London, when Deakin was shouted down and the officials were forced to leave the platform. The strikers met among themselves and said they would listen to two officials, one of them being Cousins. Cousins persuaded the meeting to vote to return to work, and Deakin never forgave him for succeeding where he himself had failed.

Deakin, who was due to retire in 1955, let it be known that Jock Tiffin was his 'favourite son'. L. H. ('Les') Pearmaine, an able official who might have been a serious contender, had left the Union some years before in protest at Deakin's authoritarian methods, and taken a job in private industry. In the election for Deakin's successor Charles Brandon, the London regional secretary, was the most hotly tipped rival to Tiffin. Cousins was named with three others as likely also-rans—Harry Nicholas, W. J. Tudor and Tom Hodgson. So little was known about him that he was described in the press as 'believed to be somewhat to the left of Deakin', and even the militant London busmen voted for Brandon, rather than Cousins, in order to try to keep Tiffin out. Cousins sought privately to get Brandon to withdraw, so that he himself could poll the maximum anti-Tiffin vote. But Brandon considered that Cousins had not yet had sufficient experience as an administrator, and declined to stand down.

The result of the election was announced in May 1955. Tiffin had a big lead with 267,019 to Brandon's 146,366. Cousins, who was not well known outside the road transport section, came a poor third with 74,217 votes.

It then became necessary to find a new Assistant General Secretary to replace Tiffin. Nominations were invited and a short list of eight was compiled. In the end the choice was narrowed to Cousins and Harry Nicholas, who was then in charge of the Union's engineering group. Nicholas was in the same age-group as Cousins and the two had been rivals all the way up the union ladder. Cousins had actually superseded him as head of the road transport section in the early 1940s. Nicholas was held by the official leadership to be more politically reliable and was generally regarded as the 'heir apparent'. When the Union's finance and general purposes committee met in August there was a dead heat. The

Chairman had given his vote in favour of Cousins.

The two candidates were called upon to appear next day before the full executive council to make a ten-minute 'impromptu' speech. A friendly official in the Union had tipped off Cousins about this ordeal, but Nicholas was apparently 'not available'. Cousins spoke passionately and his eloquence carried more weight than Nicholas's competent, though rather more cautious, approach. Cousins was elected with a two to one majority. Nicholas, whose character might be summed up as 'Handsome is as handsome does', was far too much of a gentleman to secrete the stiletto which number twos so often carry to stab their rivals in the chest. He pledged his loyalty to Cousins and has kept this pledge all his life.

Tiffin went out of his way to allay fears about the militancy of his new Assistant General Secretary. He told union members:

> I am quite certain that in the conduct of union affairs Mr Cousins will be just as left wing as the General Executive directs him to be, and no more.

During Tiffin's illness and the interregnum which followed his death, Cousins became *de facto* head of the Union, and his succession was assured. When the membership was called on yet again to elect a new General Secretary Cousins again sought out Brandon and asked whether he intended to stand. He pointed out that, having been virtually in the saddle for several months, he could be presumed to have acquired the administrative experience in which he had formerly been held lacking. Brandon, who was nearing retirement, decided not to run, and Harry Nicholas also stood down. Cousins had only one opponent—T. J. Healy, of the Farm and Flour Group. He only stood because he thought the membership should have a chance to exercise a democratic choice.

Voting took place in the spring of 1956 and the result,

announced in May, gave Cousins a landslide victory. He
polled 503,560 votes to Healy's 77,916. A bumper poll was
recorded, totalling 46 per cent of the membership. (This is a
high proportion by trade union standards. Arthur Deakin
had been elected on a 36 per cent poll. In the Amalgamated
Engineering Union, where officials are elected, not appointed,
it is rare for a candidate to poll more than about 10 per cent
of the electorate.)

The game of historical might-have-beens is always a fascinating, if pointless, exercise, and never more so than in the
affairs of the Labour movement. *If* Herbert Morrison had
become Leader of the party in 1935 instead of Attlee . . .
If Aneurin Bevan hadn't died . . . *If* Harry Nicholas had
beaten Frank Cousins for the Assistant General Secretaryship of the Transport Union—the whole history of the
Labour movement during the past fifteen years might have
looked very different.

2

A TUC within the TUC

W HEN he became General Secretary of the Transport and General Workers' Union Frank Cousins inherited a structure and a machine which were substantially the same as those originally devised by Bevin when in 1922 he welded fourteen unions into a single whole.

Since that date there have been no changes in structure, apart from minor adjustments caused by the absorption of smaller unions, or needed to match the growth of membership in particular industries. Bevin's conception was to combine geographical and occupational interests, linked through a network of interlocking committees and groups, and to forge a chain of democratic authority from the individual member through his branch to the very top. His Grand Design was conceived for about 300,000 members. Nearly forty-five years later, with five times as many members, the same pattern prevails.

Its architect was so pleased with the structure he had fashioned that when, as Foreign Secretary, he was drawing up a scheme for West European integration he planned to base it on a system of geographical and occupational groups, 'It'll be just like our union,' he said.

His successors were equally enthusiastic. Arthur Deakin, who liked to refer to the Union as his 'parish', replied to the frequent criticisms about it being too big and unwieldy. He wrote in the union journal, the *Record*, in August 1948: 'On a sober marshalling of the facts, I think we are entitled to an acquittal on the charges of overgrowth, over-centralisation, unwieldiness and irresponsibility. I believe we are entitled to maintain confidence in our structure.'

Sixteen years later Cousins boasted: 'Our members like the type of structure we are operating under.' He told the TUC in 1964 that the system which allocated members into trade groups and provided greater power at the centre matched 'the kind of thing Walter Citrine talked about when he was TUC Secretary, as the basis of future satisfactory trade union structure in the modern world'. (I very much doubt whether Lord Citrine would share Cousins' enthusiasm for his organisation, any more than he shared Bevin's.) Pointing out that the TGWU had increased its membership by 150,000 since 1948, he declared: 'We think our structure is a good reason for us doing it.'

Let us now take a closer look at this sprawling giant. Since, as we shall see in the next chapter, Frank Cousins has identified himself completely with his union, a brief description of its range and organisation is essential to an understanding of the man.

The Transport and General Workers' Union straddles across the British industrial scene, often obscuring sectional or craft interests. There is hardly a single industry, trade or occupation in which it does not have a footing. In many places, as in London's buses, it is the sole representative of the workers; elsewhere, as in the docks and road haulage, it has the overwhelming majority, and in other industries, such as the motor industry, it shares responsibility with other unions. To people in countless towns, villages and hamlets, it is 'The Union'.

The TGWU is represented on well over 300 different national and local joint negotiating bodies, including Government Whitley Councils and the Statutory Wages Councils, which determine wages and conditions for lower-paid and less well-organised workers.

The Transport and General Workers' Union might be

likened to a modern version of Robert Owen's Grand National Consolidated Trades Union of 1834, in which workers of different trades were organised in Grand Lodges, co-ordinated by a central executive. It might also be described as a TUC within the TUC.

The fundamental feature of this structure is its dual character, combining territorial and trade representation at every level.

Geographically, the Union is divided into thirteen regions. The headquarters of each (the local 'Transport House') are: London, Southampton, Bristol, Cardiff, Birmingham, Salford, Liverpool, Glasgow, Newcastle, Leeds, Hull, Belfast and Shotton (Flintshire). Each is a microcosm of the whole, and comes under a regional committee, which is elected on a territorial trade basis and is generally responsible for administration within the region. The man in charge, the Regional Secretary, is often a figure of considerable importance and influence, and some regions are very large. Region Number 1, embracing London and the Home Counties, has over 360,000 members, and if it were separately affiliated to the TUC would rank among the Big Six unions. Region Number 5, the Midlands, with 238,294 members in 1965, has been rapidly growing in size and importance with the spread of membership in the car and ancillary industries.

Industrially, members are allocated into National Trade Groups. Each of these has a nationally elected committee, drawn from the membership of the trade concerned and is served by a national group secretary at headquarters.

The basic and traditional strength of the TGWU has always lain in its dock and road transport groups. These elements have, however, been overtaken by the non-transport membership, which has been growing rapidly in engineering and in the modern industries, such as oil, petro-chemicals and atomic energy. While its primary concern is with the interests of the lower-paid workers, the Union has been in-

creasingly recruiting members among the more highly quali-
fied professional and non-manual workers.

The following table, showing the distribution of membership between various trade groups, will give some idea of the
relative strength of each:

	1964	end 1966
General workers	314,526	322,580
Engineering	269,978	268,658
Road commercial services	218,512	219,310
Road passenger services	187,787	182,432
Government workers	64,193	57,623
Chemicals	60,378	61,021
Clerical and administrative	56,541	61,881
Docks	56,104	56,129
Building	56,060	52,686
Power	40,822	43,987
Municipal workers	42,548	44,157
Agriculture	15,879	12,607
Waterways	10,712	10,437
Flour milling	15,780	15,780
Fishing	5,671	5,696

These figures include nearly 200,000 women. The TGWU
has the highest woman membership of any British trade
union.

It has always offered a home for 'odds and ends', and
people with a general desire to join a union, but with no
particular trade, are advised, 'When in doubt, join the T and
G.' Its far-flung membership includes crofters and trawler
fishermen in the Outer Islands, tomato-pickers in the
Channel Isles, and even reaches to Gibraltar, where its mixed
branch includes several hundred Spanish dockers.

For one of the more picturesque descriptions of its range I
quote Cassandra in the *Daily Mirror* (June 12th, 1958):

The roll-call reaches from silica brick workers to coffin
makers. Alongside, there are forest fire watchers and flake
maize rollermen; foremen in power houses; Admiralty

store-house men; steel benders and fat melters; foundry-
men and bricklayers; bacon curers and pin, hook and eye
operators; aerated water workers and wharf boatswains;
coal trimmers and teemers; skilled rat and mole operatives
and scaffolders; batwomen and mastic asphalt workers;
welders and the crew of floating cranes. The list is endless. . . .

If the Newmarket stableman seems somehow out of
touch with the London bus conductor on No. 23, he is
only in the same plight as a seed crusher who feels that he
is rather distant from the fifteen-year-old girl employed
in a glue and gelatine factory. Yet in Transport and
General Workers' Union theory, they are industrially one.

Cassandra made the rather cruel comment: 'Because of its
elephantine size, its complexity and its incongruous variety,
it has outgrown its strength.'

Questions of industrial 'one-ness' and internal democracy
within the TGWU are looked at in Chapter 4, but it may be
advisable at this stage to sketch briefly the way in which the
Union is governed. Without this it is difficult to understand
the position of its General Secretary.

The supreme policy-making body is the biennial delegate
conference, which is attended by about 800 delegates, elected
on the familiar regional and group pattern. The BDC does
not deal with trade subjects but debates resolutions concern-
ing 'matters of high policy and administration'. Between
times, authority is vested in the General Executive Council,
which meets quarterly and consists of thirty-nine members,
elected on a similar basis. Because this body would be too
cumbersome to exercise day-to-day control it chooses a
Finance and General Purposes Committee of eight members,
a kind of 'Inner Cabinet'. This committee meets monthly, or
more often, as necessary. Other committees deal with education, properties, the convalescent home and the superannuation fund, while members of the Executive Council, serving
in rotation, examine and appoint officers.

The basic unit of organisation is the branch, of which there are now some 5,300. These vary enormously in size and may be based on a trade or occupation, or be composite (i.e. mixed) in character. The union handbook describes the branch as 'the foundation upon which the Union is built'. 'The branch,' it says, 'is the general meeting-place of the members who, after all, *are* the Union.' Branches are obliged to meet at least once a month, and many meet more often. Their main functions are to elect representatives to serve on various committees and attend conferences, to prepare resolutions for the conferences and, in general, to discuss industrial policy.

Cousins has often declared that the Transport and General Workers' Union should aim to be 'not only the biggest, but the best' union, and should be strong administratively, as well as industrially. The TGWU is certainly big business. At the end of 1966 it reported a total membership of 1,465,662. This drop of 15,903 members, compared with the previous year, was attributed to the effects of the Government's wage freeze rather than to the union's decision in October 1965 to raise its basic contributions by 6d to 1s 9d.

The Union's income from all sources was £7¼ million, and it paid out over £1¾ million in various benefits. Its legal department recovered over £2 million in compensation and damages for members. The Union's general and other funds topped the £19 million mark at the end of 1966. All its investments are in fixed interest securities and it has refused to invest in ordinary shares, regarding it as somehow immoral to prop up a capitalist system which it is, in principle, pledged to destroy.

The Transport Union's chief rival in the field of organisation is the 800,000-strong General and Municipal Workers' Union, which is likewise an amalgamation of smaller unions, based on the old Gas Workers' Union, created in 1889. Over the years the two have built up a reasonable working relationship, both formal and informal, and by dividing up mutual spheres of interest have avoided demarcation disputes. Should any such disputes arise, both unions are obliged to invoke the TUC, whose 'Bridlington' rules govern inter-union relationships. These broadly lay down a 'first come, first served' basis, designed to protect the union which has already established itself in a particular sphere. The two general unions have often joined forces as gamekeepers against such poachers as the small Chemical Workers' Union.

The very existence of the two huge general unions, with their heterogeneous memberships, cuts right across the idea of any rational reorganisation of the British trade union movement. They are the despair of tidy-minded 'trade unionologists', who look with envy at the logical pattern of industrial trade unionism in West Germany or Sweden. They have been one of the main barriers to the development of any trend towards industrial unionism in Britain where the miners, alone, have achieved a single industrial organisation.

George Woodcock, General Secretary of the TUC, reporting in 1964 on the progress, or lack of it, towards structural reform, pronounced the funeral rites on industrial unionism. 'It is not a runner in this country and is not likely to be for the foreseeable future,' he said, after describing the protracted talks on structure between the General Council and the individual unions.

The Transport and General Workers' Union has, inevitably, been concerned in the discussions within the TUC, but its view, as we have seen, is that its own structure is bordering on perfection. Its advice to the smaller unions would be, 'Come in under our umbrella and enjoy the better service and benefits which a big union can provide.'

Cousins has always insisted that his union does not engage in take-over bids and that Big Brother does not bully or browbeat the smaller unions into surrender. At the 1964 TUC he pointed out that the TGWU works closely in transport matters with the Scottish Commercial Motormen, the United Road Transport Workers and the NUGMW. 'We do not ask them to come in,' he said. 'We sit down with them and ask about the problems of the workers and set about achieving a solution.'

In the TGWU view its peculiar horizontal and vertical structure, combining territorial and trade interests, makes it both in principle and practice the ideal vehicle for modern industrial conditions. In its written evidence to the Royal Commission on Trade Unions and Employers' Associations in 1966 the Union said it was now impossible to define an industry or isolate a craft, while it was socially and industrially wrong to separate 'white' and 'blue' collar workers. 'It seems to us that the modern union is bound to become a general one,' it concluded. Unions, it stated, ought to be large enough and have sufficient funds to provide their members with all the increasingly complex services demanded, including research, publicity, education and legal aid.

Harry Nicholas, then Acting General Secretary, was pressed to elaborate this theme when he gave oral evidence to the Royal Commission on March 15th, 1966. He outlined some of the advantages of general unions over industrial unions. 'We find with our sort of union that it is very easy for people to switch from one job to another, from one industry to another, and still preserve trade union membership,' he said. 'We get a wide experience of a great number of industries and we are able to apply that experience more effectively. . . . I believe our system is preferable to the other.'

A very important, and potentially revolutionary, development took place in the summer of 1966. The leaders of the country's three biggest unions, the TGWU, the General and Municipal Workers, and the AEU, agreed in principle to work together more closely, and set up a working committee to see how they could pool their resources and co-ordinate

c

services. In the spring of 1967 the leaders of these three unions formally agreed to co-operate in negotiations, to eliminate poaching, to recognise each other's cards, and to define each other's preserves. They also decided to co-ordinate their training and education programmes, and to look into the possibilities of streamlining contributions and benefits and methods of choosing officers.

The three unions, with a combined membership of over $3\frac{1}{4}$ million members, have denied any intention of forming an amalgamation, though this might be the logical outcome of their discussions. The numerical strength of such an organisation, and the size of its block vote, baffle the imagination. It would swamp the TUC and, some think, might render it unnecessary.

All this is very much in the future. It is time to turn back to Frank Cousins on the threshold of power.

3

Le TGWU—c'est moi

'PEOPLE talk as if this is a Cousins union. It is not a Cousins union. It is a members' union. I don't want a union of my own. I want a union of which I am the leader.'

Thus Frank Cousins once angrily brushed off the suggestion that he was a big union 'boss' or dictator. It was a typical saying, picked at random from a great many in similar vein, and it shows his complete sense of identification with his union. He is almost like Louis XIV or Charles de Gaulle in his assumption of a corporate presence and personality. A TUC colleague who accompanied him on an overseas mission for the TUC General Council remarked that Cousins always introduced himself as 'Cousins, Transport and General Workers' Union', rather than 'Cousins: TUC'.

Cousins has always had a curious habit of looking at himself from the outside and talking about Cousins as if he were a third person. 'Frank Cousins isn't important—the important thing is the Union I represent,' he has said. 'I don't care about Frank Cousins.' Once during a dock strike, when Southampton dockers had declared the *Queen Mary* 'black', Cousins went to protest to the then Minister of Labour, Iain Macleod, about a Cabinet decision to use naval tugs to get her away. 'Does the Government think they can do this to *me*?' he demanded angrily.

This attitude is not, as his critics say, a pose. It is his genuine belief that what is good for the Transport and General Workers' Union is good for the country. Because of this belief and because of his identification with the Union he has been able to dominate it from the beginning.

To be dominated by their General Secretary is no new experience for the members of the Transport and General Workers' Union. They were dominated first by Bevin, and later by Deakin. All three men were able to persuade the delegates and Executive Council members to adopt policies which they believed were right.

As a regular attender at TGWU conferences, both in Deakin's and Cousins' time, I have always been amazed at the ease with which both leaders commanded the conference. Even more amazing is the way in which union policy switched between General Secretaries. Up to Deakin's death it was consistently on the right. After Cousins took over it was equally consistently on the left.

This precise point was put to Cousins in a TV programme, 'Gallery', in May 1961. Robert McKenzie asked him if this somersault was 'a coincidence'. Cousins replied: 'I would not accept that the Union changes its policy because of a man. It changes its policy because of circumstances.'

I have sought in vain for a completely convincing answer to this problem, and have asked many people with far deeper knowledge than mine of the trade union movement for their views. I cannot say that any very satisfactory explanation has emerged, but a look at the constitutional position may throw some light.

The General Secretary is the servant of the General Executive Council, charged with 'acting generally' under its orders, and holding office 'at the pleasure of the Union'. The fact that he is the only officer to be elected (all others being appointed) gives him a unique position in the hierarchy.

National officials play no part in policy-making. They give regular reports on their stewardship to the Executive Council, and speak at conferences on their own particular subject, if called upon to do so. Within the industrial field the national trade secretaries and regional secretaries enjoy considerable autonomy and influence, but they are not entitled to air their views (publicly at any rate) on matters of policy. These are determined by the delegate conference or the General Executive Council. There is thus almost a dichotomy between the Union's political and industrial behaviour.

The General Secretary represents a continuity in what is largely a shifting population. The delegate conference meets only every other year and there is a considerable turnover of delegates, with perhaps one-third being newcomers to each conference. The General Secretary is the fountainhead not only of authority but of wisdom, and, since he is also a member of the TUC General Council, and involved in high-level talks with Ministers and employers' leaders, he is assumed to have access to facts which are denied to rank-and-file members. 'He can blind us with science,' commented one disgruntled delegate, after Deakin had held forth on the economic situation, The General Secretary is in a sense a father figure to the rank and file, and there is an element of respect for his authority. 'When Father says turn, we all turn.' This position stems from Bevin's original determination to give the Union strong centralised leadership. As Alan Bullock points out in his biography:

> The decentralised structure of the Union with the large measure of autonomy granted to the trade groups made it essential to create a strong counterpoise at the centre, if the Union was not to develop the weaknesses of a federation. The General Secretary represented the unity of the Union. . . . It was to the General Secretary that the Executive looked for guidance in formulating policy and, under his supervision, that the officers carried out the Executive's decisions.

Bullock notes: 'Few, if any, British trade unions have enjoyed such positive and powerful leadership as the Transport and General Workers' Union during Bevin's tenure of office.'

Deakin, likewise, commanded almost unimpeded authority over the Union. V. L. Allen wrote that he 'assumed the role of leader obtrusively'. Deakin had his own bulldozer methods for crushing opposition, yet he always resented the charge that he was dictatorial. 'It has been said,' he told a sectional conference in 1950, 'that I dominate the executive. That is entirely untrue. . . . Is it conceivable that I, as one individual, can dominate thirty-nine members of an executive? If I can reason with the executive, if I can give them that leadership which I am paid to give, then surely no one can fairly criticise.'

People did criticise, fairly or unfairly, and the criticisms got louder. Deakin got more indignant. He said in 1952:

> There is a disposition to mistake leadership for dictatorship. It is said sometimes that I am too forceful a personality, that I exercise too much persuasion over the constitutional bodies of the Union. I reject that statement with contempt.

In 1953, at his last biennial delegate conference before his death, Deakin secured a massive vote of confidence in himself and his politics. I wrote in the *News Chronicle*: 'Not more than half a dozen hands among the eight hundred delegates were raised when a move to censure him for his attacks on the Bevanites was put to the vote.'

At the same conference, Deakin lambasted the Labour party's plans for nationalisation. I reported: 'The eight hundred delegates listened in silence. When he asked them to accept his statement, in place of nine resolutions urging more nationalisation, not one voice was raised in opposition.'

Four years later the TGWU conference at Torquay gave Cousins a prolonged ovation when he reaffirmed his faith in the principles of nationalisation, on which his predecessor had poured such scorn. To a superficial observer the biggest difference between a Deakin-led and a Cousins-led conference was that Deakin was heard in sullen silence for the most part, while Cousins roused his audience to a fever pitch of enthusiasm.

The Union's administrative officer at the time, A. J. Chandler, wrote after the Torquay conference in the union journal, the *Record*:

> In my time I have attended many union conferences but in all sincerity I am bound to say that I have never seen a personality or a leader of men of quite the same calibre as Frank Cousins. . . . He stands high now, but one could prophesy that he will rank among the foremost trade union leaders of our history.

At Torquay I noted from the press table that Cousins had spoken at least fifty times, and twelve times on the last day. Trevor Evans wrote in the *Daily Express*: 'He runs the risk of this huge union and its conference being regarded as a one-man show. Other contributions were as watering cans to a Niagara.'

The performance was repeated at the next biennial conference, at Douglas, Isle of Man, in July 1959. This was the scene of Cousins' challenge to Gaitskell and the official Labour leadership on the H-bomb and nationalisation. His batting average—twelve speeches a day. The audience gave him the kind of rapturous reception with which teenagers today greet the Beatles. Again in 1961, though the critics were a little more vocal, Cousins swept all before him. His principal critic, Tom Fitzpatrick, a London busman, joining in the applause, declared: 'I feel like a dwarf in the shadow of a giant.' The *Sunday Times* commented: 'It seems that the TGWU politics depend upon the personal view of the man who heads its permanent machine. The majority trot comfortably in the wake of the reigning giant.'

To be fair to Cousins, he has always discouraged the excessive plaudits and personal adulation of his supporters. He accepts their bouquets, but passes them on to the Union. 'I don't believe in the cult of the personality,' he said at

Torquay in 1957. It was not his fault if Toby jugs, bearing his effigy, were on sale in the foyer of the conference hall, in aid of the Union's convalescent home. The display, however, prompted one paper to dub him 'King Toby'.

In 1959, when delegates called out for 'Three cheers for Frank Cousins' he rebuked them. 'Brothers, you should not do that,' he said. 'It is not three cheers for Frank Cousins. It is three cheers for our sane approach to this problem.'

His own attitude to leadership was defined, early on, in an interview in the *Daily Mail*:

> What you need to be a leader of men in a union is first of all a deep-seated belief in the rightness of the thing you are trying to do. You need a bit of courage to face the inevitable ups and downs. You have to recognise that people are more ready to remember your failures than your successes. And you have to learn to accept that the things you work for will only be achieved very slowly. You must not be discouraged by setbacks. You have got to believe that what you fight for will be achieved eventually.

This is a diffident statement of beliefs. It does not mean that Cousins, any more than Bevin, was not fully aware of the enormous power he wielded as leader of the nation's biggest trade union. As long ago as 1955 he told a Labour party conference: 'I represent a union that is very conscious of its power.'

When John Freeman asked him in his 'Face to Face' TV programme in October 1961: 'Do you like using power?' Cousins replied: ' "Like" is not quite the word. It is good to have power if one feels that wrongs should be remedied. But one has to be careful and responsible. . . . It is very essential to have power if the wrong is to be righted.'

Like Bevin, he has always adopted an almost paternal attitude towards his members. Bevin used to talk about 'My people', and told the House of Commons how, when he and Churchill were watching the preparations for D-Day, a soldier called out: 'See they don't let us down when we come back, Ernie.' 'Ernie?' asked a Conservative MP, who was shocked at this disrespect for one of His Majesty's Ministers. 'Yes, Ernie, that's what my people call me,' replied His Majesty's Minister of Labour and National Service.

At the big conferences of the Labour movement Cousins always stays at a modest hotel with his delegation, rather than at the more plushy four-star establishments used as official headquarters. He does so, he says, because 'my people' find it easier to come and talk to him there—and he prefers the company of the rank-and-file dockers and busmen to that of the leaders of the TUC or the Labour party. When he was Minister of Technology he said that if the Government was serious in its efforts to improve productivity 'the people we will need to talk to most and the people that will get to understand it best, will be the people I come from'. This was very much the Bevin touch.

His favourite stamping-ground has always been the smoke-laden conference hall, in some seaside resort, with its serried ranks of delegates, and he is perhaps at his happiest at his own union's periodical jamborees, known as regional festivals. These are attended by the cream, the top and most active 'brothers', who gather with their wives for a session of political evangelism, followed by tea and a cabaret.

In running a huge organisation like the Transport and General Workers' Union the man at the top inevitably has to lean very heavily on the permanent officials who constitute its civil service. Cousins' relations with his national officials have, over the years, been fairly good. He has believed in building up their authority, so that they can speak with influence at the negotiating table, and they usually have a fairly free hand. He does not like to step in to deal with a problem in a particular section, since this might undermine the authority of the individual officer.

'I have always believed that the man who is a specialist

on the job ought to be the man who is handling the job in the first instance,' he has said. 'The General Secretary only comes in if it gets too big.'

This is sound administrative practice. Arthur Deakin, some officials complained, sought to keep the reins in his own hands, with the result that he spent too much time on relatively minor matters and there was a consequent loss of efficiency. Even those officials—and there are many of them —who disagree violently with Cousins' political line have spoken of his administrative competence and fairness. 'If you drop a clanger, he'll blow you up in private, but he'll back you in public,' said one senior official.

'We can just blow into his room for a talk and take our problems to him,' said another. 'With A.D. you more or less had to make an appointment—and then you had to face the formidable barrier of getting past Ivy Saunders.' (Miss Saunders was the General Secretary's private secretary.) It would, however, be wrong to judge Deakin purely from his public or official attitudes. He was an immensely warm-hearted and generous man. If any of his officials or staff were in difficulties he would take infinite trouble to help them, and even if he lost his temper (as he frequently did) would offer a contrite apology for having done so.

On the whole, Frank Cousins was popular with his staff and his officials. When in May 1963 he had a serious heart attack and had to rest, the regrets were genuine and not just platitudinous. The union *Record* warned that his illness was 'in the nature of a danger signal'.

> Frank Cousins has never spared himself. His normal working week would frighten a lesser man. His sense of dedication to the job is such that it has been virtually impossible to persuade him to take a rest at any time.

Cousins eventually heeded the warnings of his doctor and his colleagues. He missed the Union's delegate conference in

July and only returned from a rest cure in the West Indies the following March. To squash speculation that he might be retiring on health grounds, he announced:

> I am glad to be back. I am feeling wonderfully well and looking forward to a long and fruitful experience as General Secretary. I'm still here and likely to be.

4

Grass roots

JOSEPH GOLDSTEIN, in his controversial book *The Government of British Trade Unions* (1952), examined the constitution and rules of the Transport and General Workers' Union, and reached the conclusion:

> It is evident that the government of the Union is that of a representative democracy. . . . The constitution provides a government of the membership for the membership and by the membership's elected representatives.

Over 200 pages later, having closely looked at the operations of a typical Home Counties branch and even joined it in order to get an inside picture, he wrote:

> It becomes difficult to avoid the conclusion that the Transport and General Workers' Union is an oligarchy at every level of its structure, failing to elicit the active participation of its members.

This book, not surprisingly, infuriated Arthur Deakin, who had given the author full access to union records and had even written a foreword to it. He felt that Goldstein had bitten the hand that had so generously fed him. I do not know what Goldstein would make of the TGWU in the 1960s, despite Cousins' declared aim of increasing its internal democracy. There is not much reason to suppose that the problem of apathy in the branches has been overcome, or that the membership has become any more stable than it was fifteen years ago. Goldstein found that not more than one in three members was likely to have had more than a year's membership, while not more than one in five had the necessary two years' financial qualifications to make them eligible to stand for office, paid or unpaid.

Cousins, on his election as General Secretary, was asked whether he would follow the 'Bevin' tradition or the 'Deakin' tradition. Not unnaturally, and a trifle pompously, he replied: 'I shall follow the Cousins tradition.' He early sought to embark on a process which some immediately termed 'De-Deakinisation'. He let it be known that in future there would be more militancy and more real democracy. Some of his permanent officials were bewildered at the zigzag course that was being followed, but after a meeting between Cousins and all the regional secretaries and national trade group secretaries, they were relieved to gather that they could carry on much as before.

One change which Cousins introduced was to ensure that the new General Secretary should be more easily accessible and approachable, and should descend from the Olympian heights occupied by his predecessor. Arthur Deakin had been incensed by a Vicky cartoon in the *News Chronicle* during a dock strike, showing him as a head-in-the-clouds Gulliver, striding over a swarm of Lilliputian figures and captioned: 'Rank and file, where are they?' So angry was he that he cancelled a lunch date with Mr Laurence Cadbury (the paper's chairman) and arranged for the subject to be raised in the House of Commons. This incident contributed to Vicky's departure from the *News Chronicle*.

Deakin used to deal with unofficial strikers by ignoring them and refusing to treat with their leaders. Cousins, by contrast, though he respected constitutional proprieties, was ready to meet deputations at Transport House, receiving them as members of the Union, rather than as unofficial strikers. This not only surprised the unofficial leaders but frequently took the wind out of their sails.

Two of Cousins' early attempts to inject more democracy

into the Union were to have a boomerang effect on him. One was the London bus strike of 1958, which is described in the next chapter. The other was the extraordinary incident at the Labour party conference at Brighton in 1957, during the course of the debate on disarmament and the Bomb. (His views on the Bomb are described more fully in Chapter 10.) On this occasion some of his delegation thought that he had gone far beyond the 'remit' of their delegate conference that summer, and was committing the Union to support unilateralism.

Cousins had claimed that he was speaking for his union as well as himself. This claim was immediately challenged by Charles Brandon, the doyen of the union delegation. At its Sunday morning meeting, the delegation had decided to wait and listen to the arguments from the platform before deciding which way to vote on foreign affairs. Cousins spoke before Aneurin Bevan wound up the debate, and when he returned to his seat, with the cheers of the left-wing delegates ringing in his ears, Brandon, who was sitting immediately behind him, leaned over and said: 'Frank, what on earth do you think you are doing? You know our conference decided on a multilateralist line, and you know on Sunday we decided to wait and hear what Bevan had to say.'

Peggy Herbison in the chair, seemed to be in a hurry to take the vote before the lunch break and Ted Fryer, the TGWU Chairman, who carried the union card, was preparing to raise it in support of the unilateralist resolution. 'You can't do it,' whispered Brandon, and rose to his feet to catch the chairman's eye. Cousins then strode down the aisle to the rostrum and asked Miss Herbison to delay taking the vote so that the delegation could consider their position in the light of Bevan's speech. Peggy Herbison agreed: 'This is the most vital decision that our movement is going to take,' she said, and announced that the vote would be taken at 2.15 sharp.

The Ice Rink, where the conference was being held that

year ('cold feet and hot air', as Bevan remarked) emptied rapidly. Delegates hurried back to their hotels and boarding-houses to take a rapid lunch before returning for the vital vote. Outside there was only one topic of conversation. What did Cousins mean, and which way would the TGWU vote? I rushed to the nearest phone to alert my news editor that something big was on the way.

The Transport Union delegates moved up to the gallery and had a brief, but acrimonious session. 'Can't see what all the fuss is about,' muttered Cousins, and repeated the salient points from his speech. 'Let Charlie make a statement,' said Bob Mellish, one of the Union MPs. Brandon thereupon briefly recalled the decisions of the Union's delegate confer-ence and of the delegation's Sunday meeting, and argued that Bevan's speech had cut the ground from under the feet of the unilateralists. 'This delegation has got the right and duty to decide how to vote—it is the personal responsibility of you all,' he said. No other delegate had anything to say, and the vote was taken. Though nobody divulged the figures officially, it was understood that this was in the order of sixteen to fourteen in favour of Bevan.

Later in the day a somewhat crestfallen and embarrassed Cousins called a special press conference at the Metropole Hotel. He explained that after hearing Nye Bevan the union delegation had decided to support the platform. Closely questioned, he said, 'The vote is that of the Union, not of Frank Cousins. There is nothing dramatic about being democratic.' Such a turn-down could never have happened in Deakin's day. Cousins saw to it that it never again happened in his.

Cousins became the hero of the left, but he came in for a great deal of public criticism for his assumption that the majority of his vast membership were with him on the Bomb. Possibly if a referendum had been taken the opposite would have been shown. There is a streak of chauvinism among

British working people, and opinion in the Labour movement was by no means wholly behind Hugh Gaitskell's condemnation of Suez in 1956. The idea of Britain weakening its defences did not commend itself universally to trade unionists. But no machinery exists in the TGWU, or indeed in any other union, for a referendum. The place for democratic discussion and decision is the branch, and if members do not turn up to branch meetings they have only themselves to blame if decisions of which they do not approve are carried. Many TGWU branches, moreover, feel themselves precluded from discussing subjects other than those which come into their daily field of experience.

The ordinary member of the Union has little direct contact with the leadership. Indeed, in a union the size of the Transport and General Workers' Union it would be physically impossible for the General Secretary to keep in personal touch with all the outposts of his far-flung empire. Cousins, in his first few years of office, was indefatigable in visiting the regions, attending sectional committees and conferences, meeting members and seeking to keep his finger on the Union's democratic pulse. Perhaps he remembered how Bevin had stumped the country in the early 1920s, giving lantern slide lectures on the TGWU and its functions.

In any voluntary organisation, whether it be concerned with trade unions, politics, social activities or the Church, the active minority which participates in its affairs is probably never higher than 10 per cent. The vast majority of trade unionists are content to be passive card-holders (possibly because they have to be or because they think they can get protection or benefits out of it). The Transport Union is no exception.

The main regular channel of communication between headquarters and the rank and file is the monthly union journal, the *Record*. This is an all-purpose magazine, distributed, free of charge, through branches. Enough copies are printed and distributed to supply one in every six members at an annual cost to the union of about £90,000. How many members actually read it is not known, and there is not much reason to suppose that its circulation has improved since a delegate to the 1945 conference asked:

> Is it not a fact that in many areas, the *Record* arrives month after month and is laid on the table and at the end of the month the biggest part of them have been thrown away?

This is probably the fate of most trade union journals and house magazines, especially if they are given away! I once asked a union official how much of a free hand the editor was given. 'Oh completely free, so long as he puts Frank's picture on every page,' was the reply. From time to time the Union issues special broadsheets for different sections of its membership. A potted version of the Devlin Report was circulated to the dockers, and popular versions of the 1965 and 1967 conferences were produced. This is a fairly new development, and a healthy one.

Posters and leaflets urging people to 'Join Britain's strongest Union' are produced for periodic recruiting campaigns. There is a handbook, *Your Union and You*, for new members and a special guide for shop stewards. But in spite of recent improvements it cannot be said that the TGWU makes the most of the modern media of communication. Cousins himself, until fairly recently, resisted suggestions that it would be advantageous to have a publicity department.

Cousins, like Deakin before him, attaches great importance to the Union's education scheme, which he regards as a valuable means of encouraging member interest. The scheme was originally conceived by Bevin, who said in 1939:

> We have got to create in a union like this a great bulwark of understanding in order that at all times we will have key men who understand our principles, our policy and res-

D

ponsibility and duties in order to guide the rest of our fellows.

Cousins brought in an Oxford graduate, Tony Corfield, to run it. In its evidence to the Royal Commission the Union wrote:

> We regard all our education facilities as part of our communication system and as a means of encouraging members to become active in the Union's affairs.

There is a six-part Home Study course, which explains the purpose, structure and function of the Union—in 1963-4 some 2,500 members completed the course. The TGWU also participates in the TUC education schemes and provides scholarships to Ruskin College, the London School of Economics and similar institutions.

The regions run a great many day and weekend schools, often in conjunction with the nearest university, and, for training branch officers and shop stewards—who might be called the 'cadres' or 'officer material', there is a series of courses each summer at the Royal Agricultural College, Cirencester. Branch officers are trained in speech-making, letter-writing, drafting reports and framing motions, and in the running of branch business, while shop stewards are given special instruction in the art of negotiation, in the procedures for dealing with grievances and in industrial safety.

Like most unions, the TGWU has recently expanded its education and training programmes, but, even so, these reach only a tiny proportion of the membership. (The 1965 financial report records that £29,220 was spent on education, compared with £139,435 on funeral benefits.)

In the eyes of the ordinary rank-and-file member the Union is represented by the shop steward or representative at his place of work. Union officials estimate that there are about 50,000 shop stewards and other 'activists'. The stewards operate in nearly every industry. They are key figures in workshop negotiation and can be responsible for making, or breaking, industrial peace. Yet their position in British industry is curiously anomalous. Everybody knows that shop stewards wield influence, but they are not recognised in law, nor in most unions' rule-books. Cousins has always sought to improve their status and standards and in its evidence to the Royal Commission on Trade Unions, the Union urged the need for some legal provision to secure their position and protect them against victimisation.

Shop stewards, as a genus, have got a bad name—largely because of the much-publicised excesses of a few Napoleons in the motor-car industry—but on the whole they are a hard-working and conscientious lot. Theirs is a pretty thankless (unpaid) job, collecting union subs, looking after their members' interests and taking up grievances, negotiating with managements and keeping in touch with union officials. Management, it has been said, gets the shop stewards it deserves—bad industrial relations breed trouble on the shop floor.

Apart from shop stewards, the main link in the chain of command from Transport House to the rank-and-file is provided by the Union's regional and district officials. There are now about 600 paid officers, operating in some 200 offices. The Transport Union, in fact, has a higher proportion of officers to members than most British trade unions, with nearly one to every 2,500 members. All its officers, except the General Secretary, are appointed. The argument about whether it is better to appoint or elect officers will always be an engrossing one for students of democracy. The TGWU claims that its system is superior, since it means that officials have continuity and security, and do not have to play to the gallery in the knowledge that they will have to face the electorate in a ballot. Its officers have to undergo what may be a stiff test on appointment (as we saw in Cousins' original selection as a road transport officer). They are expected not only to know about their own trades, but to be familiar with the wider aspects of industrial legislation and labour relations.

All TGWU officials are drawn from the ranks, and most have had experience as branch officials or shop stewards. Cousins once claimed:

> The so-called bureaucratic T and GWU makes a point of principle of drawing its officers from the work and the shop floor, and from the trade immediately concerned. . . . It takes pride in having created a machine from the talent thrown up in the union.

Most of the time of officials is spent on negotiations, attending branch meetings, correspondence or taking up members' grievances. They are a hard-working body of men, inadequately paid in relation to the members they serve. Salaries ranged in 1966 from the £25 a week of a junior district officer to the £1,850–£1,950 a year of a regional secretary.

There is still some element of patronage about the appointment of officials, but a good deal less than there was under Deakin. Despite the relatively low pay and the long hours of work the job is not an unattractive one, carrying a certain amount of status as well as security. Promotion prospects are reasonable in an organisation where Buggins' law of seniority is generally operative, but the majority of union officials have probably taken up the job out of devotion to the Labour movement.

In a survey of trade union officials conducted by Hugh Clegg, Fellow of Nuffield College, in 1956–9, the question was put: 'Would you like your son to become a union official?' The TGWU produced a higher proportion of officials who said 'Yes' than any other union, with 73 per cent, compared with the average of 55 per cent. Cousins' eldest son, John became an official in the Transport Union. Cousins himself once observed that he was glad John had decided to become an official, but wished he could have gone into some other union than his father's.

Senior officials, as has been noted, have very little political influence in a union which is run by the 'lay' brothers, unless it happens to be their turn to serve on a delegation to the TUC or the Labour party conference. Their industrial influence, however, is strong and even at district level an official can usually steer the proceedings at a branch meeting along the desired lines.

It is difficult, and possibly dangerous, to make generalisations about the extent of democracy within this vast organisation. Interest varies enormously, according to the trade group, the area and the issues involved. The Transport Union is probably no better and no worse than any other union. In the autumn of 1966 I made some enquiries, of a very superficial Goldstein type, at a 'composite' branch in a county town, where trade union organisation is weak and where the TGWU is the only active union. The regular attenders at branch meetings are the branch officers, and the shop stewards in the town's very limited industrial establishments (breweries, engineering, hospitals, etc.). The branch meets fortnightly and mostly does routine business, which might help account for the low attendance. A group of those who did attend regularly complained to me that they had no opportunity to discuss policy—they had not discussed the prices and incomes policy and were certainly not in favour of Cousins' line. One shop steward said:

> Most members are no more than card holders and they take very little part in the day-to-day running of the Union's affairs. . . . In my opinion, the ordinary membership is too far divorced from the central executive. The only real contact is via the *Record*, which is far from being a satisfactory journal, its correspondence pages are almost non-existent. . . . Most members would like to see the trade unions taken out of the political arena.

In general, their contact with the Union was through the district organiser, who frequently attended their branch meetings. Another member said: 'Trouble with the Union is, it's too big.'

It was difficult to judge whether these members' criticisms had been conditioned by what they had read in the press, but I felt it worth recording them—as all the group I talked to definitely came in the category of the active 10 per cent.

5

'Whoever wraps it up . . .'

MANY people, both inside and outside the Labour movement, have often complained about Cousins' unpredictability. This may apply to some aspects of his career but it is certainly not true of his attitude towards wages. His opposition to wage restraint and to any idea of Government interference in collective bargaining has been inflexible and outspoken. Indeed, he felt impelled to resign from the Labour Government rather than accept a prices and incomes policy which threatened Government control over the trade unions and on July 14th, 1966, making his first House of Commons speech from the back benches after his resignation, he recalled:

> I am on record in many places as saying that I will not have wage restraint, whoever wraps it up and brings it to me in whatever kind of parcel.

Since this attitude has been the dominating factor in his career, it is necessary at an early stage in this study of Frank Cousins to set out his philosophy on wages.

It all started at the Dome at Brighton on a sunny September morning in 1956, when Cousins was making his 'maiden' speech as his union's General Secretary at the annual Trades Union Congress. At that time the TUC policy was officially against wage restraint, but in favour of what was vaguely called 'responsibility'. Six years before, in the same hall, Congress had narrowly rejected the General Council's advice to continue the Cripps policy of wage restraint. This 1950 defeat had caused consternation among the right-wing leadership and Arthur Deakin regarded it as a great mistake. He told his union executive:

> Be that as it may, the decision having been taken, we must accept it, just as we loyally observed the previous policy which operated from 1948 to this time. However, in accepting the decision, we must also recognise that it does not mean the end of wage restraint. It simply means a shifting of the responsibility. Instead of the TUC having to accept an overall responsibility, it now becomes the responsibility of each individual trade union executive to pursue that policy of restraint best suited to the needs of its own membership.

From 1950 until his death Deakin counselled a policy of moderation in wage claims, even after the Tories had succeeded the Attlee Government in 1951. At the TUC in 1953 he violently opposed a motion sponsored by the (then) Communist-led Electrical Trades Union which declared complete opposition to wage restraint. This resolution, he said, was 'politically motivated', and it would be doing 'a great disservice to our people' to go out on a campaign for higher wages, regardless of cost. 'My own union backs me up to the hilt,' he assured delegates. The Deakin line was still broadly operative when Frank Cousins appeared on the scene, and claimed similar 'up to the hilt' backing for a diametrically opposite policy.

In a report to the 1956 Congress the General Council issued a statement which declared:

> Every trade unionist . . . has the responsibility of helping to overcome the country's economic problems. Trade unionists should be particularly conscious of that responsibility, as the preservation of full employment is bound up with the solution of those problems.

The General Council's spokesman was Yorkshire-born Wilfred Heywood, chairman of its economic committee and the general secretary of the National Union of Dyers, Bleachers and Textile Workers. He elaborated the theme of 'responsibility':

> This Congress would not, I believe, in the present temper of unions, accept a Government-introduced wage restraint brought up the back stairs. But I have sufficient faith in executive committees to believe and indeed, I think, to know, that they will act with responsibility.

Therefore, Heywood advised, all wage applications should be looked at 'prudently and sensibly, in the light of all the facts'. This was the kind of unadventurous fare to which trade union delegates had been treated at every Congress since the end of the war. Few were in a mood to be either prudent or sensible. Frank Cousins' militancy was much more to their taste.

As a member of the TUC economic committee, Cousins had taken part, during the summer of 1956, in a series of meetings with Harold Macmillan (then Chancellor of the Exchequer) and other Ministers, to discuss the critical state of the economy. He had made his views abundantly plain. But even his closest colleagues on the General Council were startled at the vehemence of his attack on the Conservative Government and its economic policies at the Brighton TUC.

He moved a 'composite' resolution (i.e. a resolution amalgamating a number of individual resolutions submitted by unions). This condemned the Government's *laissez-faire* policy and called for a return to a planned economy. Its salient phrase ran:

> Congress asserts the right of Labour to bargain on equal terms with Capital and to use its bargaining strength to protect the workers from the dislocations of an unplanned economy. It rejects proposals to recover control by wage restraint and by using the nationalised industries as a drag-anchor for the drifting national economy.

Cousins left his seat on the platform to take his place on the floor with his union delegation. As he marched up to the rostrum, clutching a sheaf of papers, a buzz of expectancy ran round the hall. What would the 'new boy' say? Like the members of the General Council, the delegates were quite unprepared for the hurricane that followed. Speaking in staccato incisive tones at a machine-gun rate of delivery which left the press corps gasping for breath, Cousins threw down the gauntlet. He elaborated the theme that the unions expected, and demanded, the right to bargain equally:

> We mean that. We assert that right. We say that we want to preserve that right. We accept that, in a period of 'freedom for all' we are part of the 'all'. When listening to Government pronouncements which talk of sharing sacrifices among us all, we sometimes wonder whether the word has a double meaning.

Then he challenged the Government:

> Let them go ahead with their 'freedom'. We have told them where it will take them. It will take them straight into the arms of the next Labour Government. But in the intervening period we are not prepared to sit down and see our members' conditions worsened. The economic prob lems in our opinion are caused by this Government.

He denied that opposition to wage restraint would neces- sarily mean a head-on clash with the Government.

> We are not going out on a rampage. We are not going to use our organisational strength to prove that the T & GWU are first and the rest can get where they like. What we are saying is that there is no such thing in this country as a place where you say, 'Wage levels stop there' and that we ought to be content, even if things remain equal.

He poured scorn on Mr Macmillan's concept of a plateau:

> This plateau of Mr Macmillan goes up and up and up. He says it will stay. Of course it will, if we do nothing

about wages. If he can balance his economy at the expense
of the workers, it will stay.

And in a side-swipe at the Chancellor's rather wistful remark
that he would like to be invited to the TUC, he said: 'What
does he think the TUC is—a film festival?'

Cousins sat down to thunderous applause. A brief debate
followed which the miner's leader Arthur Horner described
as 'not so much a debate, more a demonstration'. In his
reply Cousins wound up with a warning:

> No union leader, whether of a big or a little union, wants
> to throw his gauntlet down and turn round to see who
> picks it up. That is not the issue. It has been thrown down.
> We have said we do not want it, but if it is there we will
> not refuse to pick it up if we are compelled to.

The Chairman, Sir Thomas (now Lord) Williamson,
announced that the General Council supported the motion,
and a forest of hands shot up in the hall. The members of the
General Council did not join in the general jubilation. They
had decided after hasty consultation amongst themselves not
to oppose a resolution which was so patently going to be
carried, and they sat glum and grim-faced, while delegates
cheered their heads off.

Later, at lunchtime at the Metropole Hotel, the 'Old
Guard' of the TUC expressed great alarm at the implications
of the vote, and at the likely consequences of Mr Cousins.
He had, in their view, issued a direct challenge to the Government which threatened to unleash forces which could not be
controlled. Above all, there was concern about the political
implications of his speech. Cousins had himself said: 'A
motion of this nature must of necessity be political.'

The intrusion of politics, and Labour party politics at that,
ran counter to the private hopes of some union leaders that
the TUC would become increasingly a-political and loosen
its formal links with Labour. Sir Vincent Tewson, then

General Secretary of the TUC, had said when the Conservatives won the 1951 election that the TUC would seek to work 'amicably' with the new Government. For all the difficulties, and largely thanks to Arthur Deakin, this was the course which they had steered over the past five years. 'Disastrous' was the general reaction to Cousins' speech, while some union leaders predicted a period of industrial strife and a weakening of foreign confidence in the pound.

By and large, the press shared the General Council's views, though all commentators agreed that a new epoch in trade union history had begun. Hannen Swaffer wrote in the *People*: 'Suddenly he has become the most powerful man in Britain.' The *Daily Mail* warned that the Transport Union's new boss would 'wreck and ruin national prosperity for a political motive'. Trevor Evans in the *Daily Express* wrote: 'This is the morning after at the TUC—the morning after Mr Frank Cousins, the powerful new chief of the T and GWU, had grabbed the steering wheel of the whole TUC and swerved it violently to the left.'

The events of the Brighton 1956 TUC were decisive both for Frank Cousins and for the Labour movement. For Cousins it represented a moment of triumph and a taste of success such as he probably never experienced, before or after. Within a few months of taking office he had managed to swing the entire Trades Union Congress behind him in a speech which many still regard as the most effective he ever made. He had demolished a decade of co-operation with the Government and broken decisively with the Deakinite policies of moderation. Many on the left would have agreed with Frank Foulkes, the then President of the Electrical Trades Union, when he declared: 'A new light is shining in the trade union movement.'

From 1956, with unfailing regularity, Cousins made much the same speech at every conference of the TUC and the Labour party. It would be tedious to follow him on the conference merry-go-round between Brighton and Blackpool, for to re-read these speeches is to experience variations on a theme, with more theme than variations. The theme was always the same—no wage restraint, no Government interference in collective bargaining and the return of a Labour Government pledged to genuine economic planning. Sometimes this was backed with a threat of industrial action. Thus, at the Blackpool TUC in 1957, he said:

We should be prepared to take every step through negotiation and, if appropriate, through reference to arbitration, but we shall also reserve our right as an organisation to withdraw labour. . . . We are not calling anybody's bluff—we are not bluffing either.

In this speech he poured scorn on Mr Macmillan's idea for a kind of super wages committee or court to advise the Government on wage and salary movements:

We think that our traditional way in this country of negotiation with employers without Government instruction or direction is the appropriate one. . . . If the Government want a committee to advise them, that is their affair. We, from our union, do not want a committee to advise us how to handle the affairs of our members' interests. We have a committee: our General Executive Council.

The Macmillan proposal had first been mooted at a meeting at the Treasury in July 1957. Cousins had embarrassed his colleagues by asking Peter Thorneycroft (who had succeeded Mr Macmillan as Chancellor in January): 'What would your reaction be if the TUC ignored any report made by this independent body?' Such direct speech to Cabinet Ministers was regarded as approaching *lèse-majesté*, and the General Council decided by fifteen votes to nine to 'note' the Government's intentions and reserve its position.

The Cohen Council on prices, productivity and incomes, popularly known as the 'Three Wise Men', was duly set up in

August, and in December Cousins led a minority in the
General Council against accepting an invitation to meet Lord
Cohen. Not for the first, or last, time, he found that his line
was eventually adopted by the TUC. The following summer,
the General Council told Lord Cohen: 'It would serve no
useful purpose to have a further meeting.'

The whiplash of Cousins' tongue was directed against
Selwyn Lloyd who became Chancellor in 1961 (the Conservatives had no fewer than six different Chancellors between
1955 and 1962). Selwyn Lloyd had introduced his policy of a
pay pause, followed by a 'guiding light', with a norm for
increases of $2\frac{1}{2}$ per cent. For all the furore the pay pause
created, the Selwyn Lloyd measures were not nearly as savage
as the Wilson standstill of 1966, but the TUC was roused to
anger at the Government's interference with the 'normal processes of collective bargaining' and industrial arbitration. A
delegate at the TUC conference in Blackpool in 1962 commented: 'We have had four or five really rough Chancellors
since 1951, but this fellow strikes me as being the roughest
and toughest of them all.'

At this conference Cousins moved a 'composite' resolution
of inordinate length and verbiage, even by TUC standards.
It condemned the Tory Government policies and the Selwyn
Lloyd pay pause, the guiding light and the Government's
proposal to establish a National Incomes Commission (NIC
or 'Nicky') in succession to the 'Three Wise Men'. The TUC
had decided, this time without reservations, to boycott
'Nicky', regarding it as 'one-sided and irrelevant'.

In a statement to the Congress, which read as if it might
have been drafted by Cousins himself, the General Council
said:

> The Government's proposal to establish a National
> Incomes Commission can only confirm the nation's belief
> that the Government is casting about desperately for some
> means of reprieving its misguided incomes policy, and of

extricating itself from the spreading disapproval of its general economic policies.

'Nicky', in fact, made barely a ripple on the economic scene and disappeared, unloved and unlamented, some years later—though some said it had paved the way for the Labour Government's National Board for Prices and Incomes.

The National Economic Development Council, popularly known as 'Neddy' was a very different matter. Here the TUC accepted that such a body could play a positive part in planning for economic expansion and, with only a few dissentients, had decided to co-operate. Cousins, who was one of the six TUC men chosen to serve on the NEDC said in 1962: 'My union is now proud that we are associated with it.'

The emphasis in his speech to the TUC was on the need for a Labour Government which would follow a policy of planned expansion and achieve a fairer distribution of national wealth. He made an important statement of his policy:

> In our approach to planning, in our request for co-ordinated effort on the part of the unions and the setting down of what the policies for expansion really are, there should be no misunderstanding about why. We want a new system designed to create, instead of 'free-for-all', 'Fair for all'; and when this is there, we shall be with it.

He added, somewhat cryptically: 'Those who are so glibly now saying that a new Cousins is emerging want to recognise that it was not Frank Cousins who said this, but the General Council who said it to the Government and made public an announcement of the need for planning at the last Budget period.' His 'We shall be with it' promise led to widespread hopes that, if and when a Labour Government was returned to power, Cousins and his union would co-operate in operating an incomes policy. In 1963, when Labour was forging ahead in the opinion polls and a general election seemed imminent, Cousins' speech to the Brighton TUC appeared to confirm these hopes. The General Council had issued an economic statement which implicitly accepted the need for an incomes policy and TUC General Secretary George Woodcock had put the blunt question: 'Will trade unionists be able to assert that everything else can be planned except wages?'

The TGWU vote was cast in favour of Woodcock's statement, and Cousins went so far as to say:

> When we have achieved a measure of planning and a Socialist Government, and if I have to say to my members 'We must now exercise restraint', I will say it, and when I say it, I will mean it.

At the same time, he supported a resolution moved by Ted Hill, the left-wing leader of the Boilermakers' Society, declaring 'complete opposition to any form of restraint'. Cousins explained:

> It is no good anyone pretending that, however much we disguise it, we as a trade union movement will be party to wage restraint, however much we equivocate about the intention and meanings of words.

He indignantly denied criticisms that, in both accepting the General Council's report and voting for Ted Hill's motion, he was guilty of duality.

A month later, when the Labour party conference met at Scarborough, Cousins backed a resolution on economic policy and planning for full employment which called, among other things, for 'an incomes policy to include salaries, wages, dividends and profits (including speculative profits) and social security benefits'. He explained his motives for supporting this policy:

> I hope, on behalf of my Union, and I hope every other trade union in this country, we can say to the Labour Party: 'We will support you in your intentions. We will vote for

The future Transport Union chief.
These photographs were taken in
Yorkshire about the time the young
Frank Cousins left the pit to
become a lorry driver

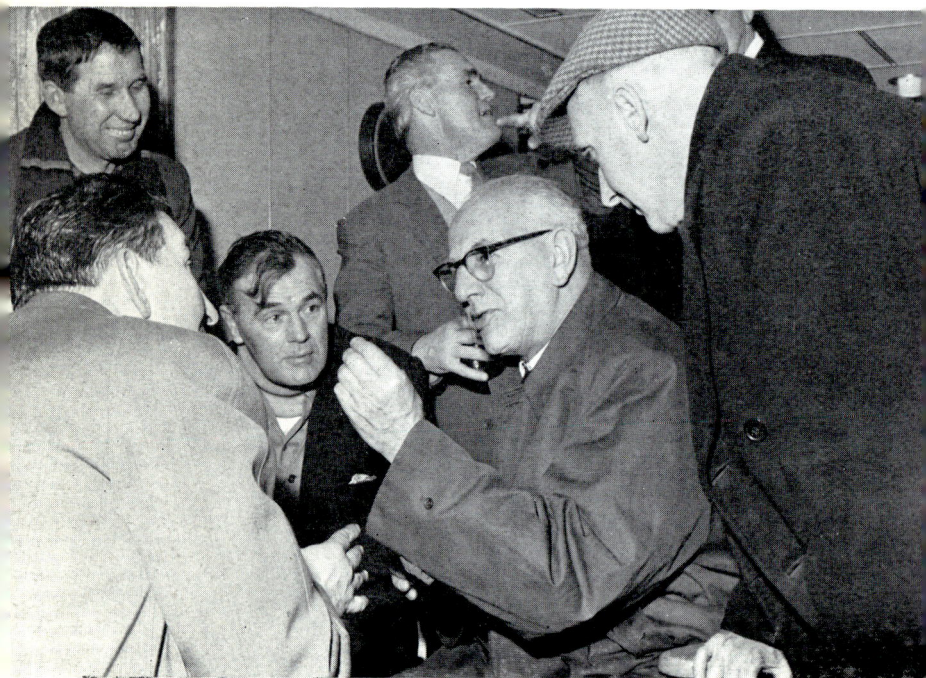

The General Secretary and members. *Above:* London busmen on the eve of the strike rally, May 1958. *Below:* With a group of dockers at Millwall Docks, spring 1967

this resolution because we think your intentions can be displayed within the context of this resolution.'

He made it plain, however, that he did not accept that the term 'incomes policy' included wage restraint.

> We are spending a good deal of time ensuring that we get a Government that thinks the same things as we do, and when we have succeeded in getting that Government, we shall be talking as we are now, about a planned growth of wages, not wages restraint.

Events did not turn out as he, and many others, expected. The development of Labour's prices and incomes policy is described in a later chapter, but it is important to stress at this stage that Cousins was never committed unconditionally to support any policy which did not conform to his own interpretation.

6

'We don't like strikes, but . . .'

Cousins' speech to the TUC at Brighton in 1956, in which he demolished the concept of wage restraint, was widely interpreted as a challenge to the Government. It certainly touched off a series of industrial explosions. Members of the Transport and General Workers' Union were involved in strikes in the motor industry and in the national engineering stoppage of March 1957 and there were strikes of provincial busmen, dockers and market porters. It seemed that Britain was entering its worst period of industrial unrest since 1926.

Cousins was able to avert a number of stoppages, or at least to nip some of them in the bud. In January 1957 he talked the London busmen out of a strike threat. In February he intervened in a dispute at Fords' Dagenham works and in April he managed to get the London tally clerks to settle their grievances peacefully. He hurried back from a caravan holiday in Devon in the summer to tackle a strike of Covent Garden porters and succeeded, where the London officials had failed, in getting the men back on terms they had originally rejected. For the first time since he became General Secretary Cousins, who had been basking in his supporters' adulation, tasted unpopularity. After a meeting at Friends House, where he won a five to four majority for a return to work, angry strikers crowded round him, calling out: 'Liar', 'Judas' and similar epithets and advising him: 'Take another holiday'. He was offered, but refused, a police escort to his car.

As a result of all this, he acquired something of a reputation as an industrial statesman. It is strange to find the *Daily Mail* welcoming his 'strong leadership tempered with wisdom' and commenting: 'Mr Cousins has done more to maintain industrial peace than anyone else in the world.'

The situation changed completely after the London bus strike of May 1958. From being hailed as a peace-maker, he was pilloried as the villain who held London to ransom and threatened to plunge the whole nation into chaos. Both versions are wide of the mark. Cousins is neither trigger-happy nor an appeaser. He upholds the strike weapon as a last resort to enforce his belief in what is right, but he has never been in favour of its indiscriminate use. He told the TUC in 1957:

> We don't like strikes because they are not the most intelligent way of dealing with problems, but there are occasions when you have to show people that you mean it.

During the national engineering strike of March 1957 he said:

> There is no virtue in striking for striking's sake, but there is virtue in winning this strike.

Unlike the 'Apprenti Sorcier', he has always been chary of unleashing forces which he cannot control. He assured his union conference at Torquay in 1957 that there was no intention of embarking on industrial strife just to show the Union's strength. 'We have no wish to say to the country "Feel our muscles",' he said.

The TGWU attitude towards strikes has remained consistent. In its evidence to the Royal Commission in 1966 it said: 'The right of a man to withdraw his labour is an essential freedom which cannot, and ought not to be impaired.' It pointed out that workers who strike often suffer considerable sacrifice and argued: 'The only really sensible method is to look at the circumstances in which disputes occur.' Many strikes were caused or prolonged because employers refused to operate agreed procedure or showed 'incompetence, ill-temper or failure in communications'.

Frank Cousins soon found to his cost that it was in practice extremely difficult to reconcile democracy with discipline. His members had for so long been subjected to authoritarian leadership that reactions to a more tolerant regime were, not surprisingly, excessively enthusiastic. To the vast majority the change of leadership probably made no difference, but the left-wing minorities made the most of it.

The London busmen have always included a highly militant section—as Bevin found when he was faced with the Communist-led 'Coronation Strike' in 1937. Originally, this strike received official support, but it developed beyond the point where it could be controlled by Transport House. Nearly twenty years later the militants were again able to force the pace. One of them recently told me: 'We deliberately set out to enmesh Cousins. We got him involved in all our negotiations and brought him to the point of no return.' He added: 'Since then Frank has kept out of our way as much as he can.'

The London bus strike of May 1958 provided Cousins with his biggest and most exacting test as a union leader. This is not the place to tell the full story of those seven gruelling weeks, but the strike formed such an important chapter of his career that it is essential to recall some of the main events.

Trouble with London Transport had been brewing during the greater part of 1957, though Cousins had dissuaded the men from strike action in January. The issue flared up again in the autumn, soon after the settlement of a provincial bus dispute, and the London men decided, against the advice of the union leaders, to go ahead with a claim for an increase of £1 5s a week. Cousins and Harry Nicholas had planned a concerted approach on behalf of all bus workers, so as to prevent the leap-frogging of their claims. The Londoners' unilateral action cut right across these plans for umbrella

negotiations. The men at first rejected the official advice to go
to arbitration, but later, on Cousins' persuasion, they reversed this decision and agreed to refer the dispute to the
Industrial Court, while keeping the strike threat in reserve.

In March 1958 the court, under Sir John Forster, recommended an increase of 8s 6d for 36,000 London crews, with
nothing for the 14,000 London Transport's country and
Green Line crews or its maintenance workers. This award
was rejected contemptuously by a delegate conference of very
angry busmen, and Cousins commented that the men were
'perfectly justified in reaching this conclusion'.

The London Transport Executive, meanwhile, accepted the
award and refused to improve on it. 'We will apply the award,
the whole award and nothing but the award,' insisted its
Chairman, Sir John Elliot. To this Cousins retorted: 'If that
is your position, then we shall fight, and we shall win.'

Cousins undoubtedly did his utmost to prevent the strike
and seek a reopening of negotiations. No doubt he remembered Bevin's dictum, 'Never strike if you are on weak
ground.' The London busmen's cause was hardly a popular
one, but he was caught between the Scylla of their militancy
and the Charybdis of Government policy. All last-minute
efforts to find a peace formula failed and Cousins announced:

> We have to enter upon a grim struggle. The Union has
> made every effort to arrive at a just settlement and has
> acted with tolerance and restraint. We are now left with no
> alternative but to take the extreme course of withdrawing
> our labour.

He had been infuriated by an earlier decision of the
Government to veto the idea of a committee of inquiry into
bus pay and conditions. This had been suggested by Sir
Wilfred Neden, the Ministry of Labour's chief industrial com-
missioner (with his Minister's knowledge and approval).
Cousins called formally at 8 St James's Square to ask the

Minister: 'Is this your decision or that of the Government?'
Iain Macleod, then the Minister, admitted that he had consulted with his senior colleagues. Cousins became convinced
that the Ministry, no longer a free agent, would be precluded
from operating its normal conciliation procedures. As he saw
it, the London busmen were the sacrificial victims of the
Conservative Government's wage policy. At no stage, however, did he harbour any unconstitutional motives. In a statement during the strike he said:

> Although directly opposed to the present economic
> policy, we recognise that it is the policy of the elected
> Government. We accept without question that it is the
> Government's duty to govern, and it is not our desire, as a
> union, to seek to usurp any functions of Government.

The strike, which had received the necessary formal sanc-
tion from the General Executive Council, was launched at a
mass meeting of 5,000 London busmen at the Empress Hall,
London, on Friday, May 2nd. A resolution pledged overwhelming support for 'a fight to the finish'. A Wandsworth
driver, Mr Harry Parker, was quoted in the *News Chronicle*
as saying: 'Cousins is the finest leader this union has ever
had.' Another busman, who not surprisingly chose to remain
anonymous, reported: 'Many of us are dead against this
strike.'

Once the die was cast, Cousins threw everything he had
into the battle, which he regarded as a test case for the entire
Labour movement. The appeals to working-class solidarity
met with an enthusiastic response, and the opening days of
the strike, which began at midnight Sunday, May 4th, un-
rolled in an atmosphere not unlike that of the General Strike,
thirty-two years earlier. (Why is it that the month of May so
often seems to coincide with Labour unrest?)

The TUC General Purposes Committee on May 7th gave
the busmen its unequivocal blessing and launched a national

appeal for funds, to which many unions responded generously. The strike was 100 per cent solid, the pickets at London
garages saw to it that no potential strike-breaking bus could
be slipped through their lines. The London Underground and
railway workers, who belonged to the railway unions, were
told to carry on normally, but not to man any extra trains or
undertake any additional duties which might be regarded as
strike-breaking.

The dispute dragged on and by the time it entered its
fourth week neither side showed any signs of breaking. Nor
were there any signs of a move from the Government. Mr
Macleod said he was waiting for 'a chink of light', to which
Frank Cousins replied, 'He wants to be careful his chink
doesn't develop into a conflagration.' A threat of a national
stoppage of railwaymen came and went, and the busmen
were very angry at the Government's speedy intervention in
the rail dispute, compared with its dilatory attitude towards
their own stoppage.

The Union was already beginning to feel the effects of the
drain on its funds, for the strike was costing about £200,000 a
week in strike pay alone. Faced with the prospects of a war of
attrition, the militants began to exert pressure on the leaders
to spread the conflict. They urged that other, decisive, sections of the Union should be brought in, so that private
coaches could be cut off from their supplies of petrol and
London's Underground starved of current. This, they argued,
would soon bring Sir John to his knees and London to a
standstill. Towards the end of May there was thus a very real
possibility that the strike of 50,000 London busmen might
develop into a major national stoppage. This was too much
for the TUC General Council, which rapidly developed cold
feet and forgot its earlier enthusiasm for the busmen's cause.
A series of emergency meetings was held, to see whether there
was any chance of reopening negotiations, and on June 4th,
after a meeting which lasted five and a half hours, Cousins

was flatly told by the General Council not to spread the strike. The official statement runs:

> The General Council decided to advise the Transport and General Workers' Union against any extension of the stoppage to other groups of workpeople.

The TUC leaders met in the knowledge that the Government meant business. It had cancelled the leave of 6,000 Army drivers and had issued a warning to motorists not to use their cars unnecessarily. Outside the meeting at Congress House strikers paraded with banners and posters proclaiming: 'TUC traitors—underlings—cowards' and 'TUC kills trade unionism'.

Not for the first, or by any means the last, time Frank Cousins found himself isolated. Alone the Communist-led Electrical Trades Union pledged positive action to 'cut off the juice' and stop the Tubes. The London *Star* commented: 'Cousins is becoming daily more desperate.' But Trevor Evans in the *Daily Express*, wrote: 'Cousins may go through Hell, but he will be back with a Bang. Why? Because most of his mistakes have come from being too near the people he leads.'

The public was becoming increasingly hostile to the Transport Union and impatient with the Government's inertia. People were also getting extremely bored with the acrimonious and petulant exchanges between Cousins and Sir John Elliot, and regarded both men as obsessively obstinate. The NUR rejected a direct appeal from the busmen to let its Tube drivers join the strike, and there were some rumblings of discontent among busmen and their families. 'This strike is a flop, London is managing,' declared Sir John. Cousins himself showed signs of despondency, as the dice seemed weighted against him and the financial situation grew more desperate. It looked as if the Union might have to sell some of its securities to finance the strike.

On June 6th he managed to persuade the men to accept the TUC's advice, and by seventy-one votes to sixty a delegate conference rejected a call to extend the strike, though it agreed to carry on the limited London stoppage. At Oxford on June 8th Cousins told a regional meeting:

> London busmen will go it alone, if necessary till Christmas. They came out, they are out and they will stop out.

It was during this weekend at Oxford that Cousins found out how a public figure can expect no private life. Reporters from a national paper descended on the Randolph Hotel, where he had been staying with his wife and union officials, and gleefully produced and paraded the bill in Monday morning's paper.

At last, as the strike entered its sixth week, the Minister of Labour decided that things had gone on long enough and discovered a convenient 'chink of light'. Talks were reopened under his auspices and after some days a possible settlement emerged. London Transport promised that the country busmen would get an increase 'not substantially less' than that of the London crews. It did not seem a very generous concession, but it was certainly represented as such, and enabled the Union to recommend a return to work without loss of face.

On June 13th a delegate conference on a three to one vote decided: 'To continue the struggle would not be in the interests of the members, in view of the forces ranged against us.' A last-minute hitch arose through a rather inept circular posted by London Transport in its garages, and the branches voted, narrowly, to stay out. This was the last kick of democracy. The difficulty was cleared up and a week later the branches voted overwhelmingly to end the strike. On June 20th, after forty-nine days' absence, the red buses were back on London's streets.

The London bus strike was described at its outset by Sir

John Elliot as 'the strike nobody can win'. At the end, almost in the tones of a BBC commentator on a football final, he said: 'The strike has ended honourably. I regret talk of Victory or Surrender. Neither side has surrendered its belief in its principles.' To stress his magnanimity, he presented each member of the busmens' negotiating committee with an autographed copy of his book on the French Revolution, *The Way of the Tumbrils*.

For all the final courtesies, the London bus strike left a great trail of bitterness in its wake. It cost the busmen about £4 million in lost earnings and the Union over £1 million in strike pay. London Transport not only lost heavily in revenue but suffered permanent damage in declining traffic from which, eight years later, it had still not recovered.

Cousins' final comment on the strike: 'We can be very proud of the 50,000 men and women who stopped work in the knowledge that they started the strike for 14,000 other people and not for themselves.' He himself emerged from the conflict with his reputation enhanced on the left. Geoffrey Goodman commented in the *Daily Herald*: 'Cousins is stronger than ever'. But most observers thought that his public reputation had suffered and many believed that the strike contributed to the Labour party's defeat in the 1959 election. Cousins' relations with the press were not improved, and he was particularly bitter about the TUC General Council's attitude.

The Times, which considered that he could have got as good terms for his busmen much earlier, without the strike, and had allowed the men's negotiating committee to overrule him, wrote: 'He seemed to see himself as a sort of Prometheus defying the Gods of the Establishment on behalf of ordinary men.'

7

The cat that walks alone

COUSINS' political and industrial influence might have been greater, and more positive, if he had enjoyed—or cultivated—better relations with his colleagues on the TUC General Council. A graph of these relations would show violent fluctuations but, over the years, the dominant atmosphere has been one of mutual suspicion

When he first joined the General Council in February 1956 there was a great deal of goodwill towards him and a general desire to help him as a relatively inexperienced newcomer. The goodwill diminished when Cousins rebuffed these overtures and made it quite clear that he needed no help in running his union, or representing its interests. Senior members recall how, within a few weeks of his joining the General Council, he was 'laying down the law' and they not unnaturally resented what they regarded as presumption. He was immediately co-opted on to the key economic committee, a position usually reserved for union leaders with long service, and thus reached a seat of power within the TUC without having to serve an apprenticeship.

The alarm and despondency with which the more orthodox members of the General Council viewed his speech to the Brighton TUC in 1956—his 'maiden' speech as a General Secretary—have already been described. They got their revenge a few days later by nominating him as official spokesman to oppose a resolution calling on the TUC to launch a national campaign for an immediate forty-hour week.

Cousins performed this chore half-heartedly, and the General Council was defeated by a four to three majority. 'It seems to me that Mr Cousins is a reluctant, yet obedient, member of the General Council,' quipped Jim Jarvie, the leader of the tiny Associated Blacksmiths, Forge and Smithy Workers, who had moved the successful resolution.

From 1956 onwards the principal objective of many TUC leaders was to 'contain' Frank Cousins. They knew they could neither 'nobble' him nor squash him. Their task was made difficult by Cousins' own unpredictability. In Arthur Deakin's day everybody knew which way the TGWU vote would go on every issue and whom he would support for various positions in the Labour movement. With Cousins it was usually guesswork.

The TUC and the Labour party follow different electoral procedures. The General Council now consists of thirty-five members, who are elected by the entire Congress each year, but each of the nineteen trade groups nominate their own candidates. In most groups, such as railways, transport, textiles, and agriculture, the nominees of the dominant unions are elected unopposed. In some, as for example the Civil Service, and non-manual workers' groups, there is keen competition for a single place, and the candidate who can rely on the support of the Transport and General Workers' Union starts with a considerable advantage.

This system has frequently been criticised and there are regular attempts by the smaller, or white-collar unions, to change the rules, so as to limit each trade group to electing its own representatives. These efforts have always been frustrated by the big unions which like the *status quo*, and argue that members of the General Council are there to represent the whole movement, and not sectional interests. The result is a perpetuation of the predominance of the manual workers, even from declining industries like railways, coal-mining and textiles, and an under-representation of the growing numbers in non-manual occupations and in the newer technological industries.

Competition for a seat on the Labour National Executive is more open, and engenders more excitement. Twelve places are allotted to trade union representatives and these are usually filled by the nominees of the bigger unions. The trade unions have no voice in the election of the seven constituency representatives. These are chosen directly by the constituency delegates from a long list of candidates, with sometimes three or four times as many names as there are seats. Strong political animosities are aroused and during the 1950s the capture of the National Executive by the Bevanites was generally attributed to a carefully organised campaign in the constituencies under the generalship of Ian Mikardo. The party Treasurer and the five women members are elected by both the trade union and the constituency sections. The Party Leader and deputy leader are *ex-officio* members, and there is one representative of the Co-operative movement (usually unopposed). The trade unions thus dominate the voting for eighteen seats on the NEC.

Arthur Deakin had used his power uninhibitedly. For both the TUC General Council and the Party National Executive he supported only those whom he regarded as politically 'reliable'—and that meant candidates who would support Deakin policies. Mrs Eirene White, MP, was an early victim. She decided in 1953 to withdraw from the contest for the women's section of the National Executive because, she said, 'I have good reason to think that the leaders of some of the larger unions have decided that a person of my moderate views is not acceptable to them on the executive.' It was impossible, she declared, to hold a middle-of-the-road course between 'the bludgeons of the right and poisoned arrows of the left'. Deakin's laconic comment: 'I care neither what Mrs White says, nor what she does.'

There was not the same deliberate use of the massive union

vote with Cousins. He disliked the idea of horse-trading and openly said that he would support people on their merits, irrespective of their policies.

This worked as a general rule, though it was noticeable that in 1958 the TGWU switched their vote in the women's section from the right-wing Dr Edith Summerskill to the left-wing Jennie Lee. Arthur Horner, the Communist miners' leader, who on sheer ability deserved a place at 'the top table', failed to receive the Union's support. In 1956, when there was a bitter contest for the party treasurership between Aneurin Bevan and George Brown, the TGWU vote was cast for Brown, as one of its members, and irrespective of the political preferences of its General Secretary.

Sir Tom O'Brien, the ebullient leader of NATKE, the theatrical and film workers' union, was left in an annual state of suspense until the results of the ballot for the General Council were announced, wondering whether he would get the TGWU vote. He always did in the end, but there would often be quite sharp exchanges within the TGWU delegation when it was considering the list. Some left-wingers wanted to drop O'Brien, but Cousins, who is at bottom a kind-hearted man, always came out in his favour. Until the results of the ballot were announced, half-way through the conference, Sir Tom would be like a cat on hot bricks. Afterwards he would be his own rumbustious self and, as like as not, call for drinks all round.

The London bus strike of May 1958 marked the nadir of Frank Cousins' relations with most of his General Council colleagues. On his side there was smouldering anger at the way in which he felt he had been let down. On their side reactions ranged from pious hopes that he would now settle down and become a comfortable conformist to wilder jubilations that at last Cousins had been 'cut down to size'. Few regarded the outcome of the strike as anything but a defeat for him.

On the eve of the Bournemouth Congress in September
the General Councillors who were assembling in the Grand
Hotel were uneasy, wondering what was going on at a small
establishment up on the cliffs, some way out of town. They
feared there might be an explosion if Cousins decided to rally
the left in an onslaught against the General Council's report
on the bus strike, which would be presented to the delegates.
In the event, and much to their relief, the volcano did not
erupt.

On the second day of the conference John Burns, President
of the Fire Brigades Union, sought to fan the flames. 'This
report suggests to me that we have landed in the drawing-
room of Carlton House,' he said. 'It is a document which
would have been far better put before the Primrose League.'
He accused the TUC leaders of being 'more concerned with
respectability than with social revolution'. He was backed by
Frank Haxell, the Communist secretary of the Electrical
Trades Union, who protested that the TUC ought to have
mobilised the combined forces of the Labour movement
against the combined forces of the Government and the
employers in support of the busmen.

This was certainly a good militant launching-pad for
Cousins, and there was an atmosphere of tense expectancy as
he left his seat. But he was in a conciliatory mood and was
clearly not anxious to get tarred with the extreme left-wing
brush. He thanked all the unions who had given generous
financial and moral backing to the busmen, and urged that
there should be no inquest on the strike. 'Do not get too
deeply involved in a debate on this report,' he appealed.

Sir Vincent Tewson, the TUC General Secretary, declared
that the General Council had no apologies to make, and paid
tribute to the busmen's magnificent fight. There the matter
ended, on a note of anticlimax from which the conference
never recovered. Whether it was the relaxing air of Bournemouth, or a hangover from the bus strike, the 1958 Congress

will surely be remembered as the most torpid in the whole of trade union history. Publicly, the hatchet was buried. Privately, it took a long time to forgive and forget.

During the late 1950s Cousins cut a lonely figure on the General Council. He could often count his supporters on the fingers of one hand. The Transport and General Workers' Union had two other representatives on the Council and they would usually look to see which way their General Secretary was voting and vote the same way. Even Dame Florence Hancock, one of the two women members and a former TUC Chairman, was impelled to toe the line when it came to the vote, though all her instincts would have been with the right-wing.

Ted Hill, the rough-hewn leader of the boilermakers, was far out on the left, and so was John Newton, Secretary of the Tailors' and Garment Workers' Union. On such issues as the Bomb or nationalisation they were generally in the Cousins camp. Sometimes Robert Willis, the printers' leader, who was no respecter of persons or position, would back him, but there was nothing cut and dried about it. There was no Cousins clique and no automatic alignment of a Cousins-led group against the TUC 'Establishment'. At times Cousins would vote with the majority and leave his erstwhile allies wondering what had happened.

On at least two occasions the 'rebels' sought to make common cause with him and invited him to talk things over privately. Both times he accepted, but failed to turn up. The first time, in the clubroom opposite the Congress House, which was the rendezvous of the more gregarious members of the General Council, Cousins stayed talking to journalists, while the three would-be nonconformists stood disconsolately on their own. The second time, he failed to turn up to an evening date at the London flat of one of the three. He obviously did not wish to be identified with the 'outer circle' and harboured an almost pathological fear of being 'used'. He

Back at Union Headquarters after resigning from the Government. With Harry Nicholas, Assistant General Secretary, and Jack Jones, Assistant Executive Secretary

Above: With Hugh and Dora Gaitskell at Scarborough, October 1960. Standing, Len Forden, union chairman. *Below:* The Aldermaston marcher

judged issues, as he judged people, on their merits.

His aloofness and intolerance were hardly calculated to make friends, even if they could influence people. He was, to say the least, an awkward and uncomfortable colleague, and life on the General Council had become rather like living on the slopes of Mount Etna. No doubt his fellow councillors would agree with the French proverb which Maurice Edelman, Labour MP for Coventry North, dug out: '*Cousinage dangereux voisinage*'. There was a strong undercurrent of jealousy at the blaze of publicity in which he moved, and the frequency of his appearance on TV. There was also considerable resentment at the apparent assumption that he and his union were the fount of all trade union knowledge and wisdom, and that his massive block vote somehow vested him with special privileges. No doubt his contemporaries felt the same about Bevin.

There was a significant incident in the autumn of 1963, when the TUC International Committee was choosing a new chairman. The result was a dead heat—five all—between Cousins and Fred Hayday, of the General and Municipal Workers' Union. The line-up is interesting. The pro-Cousins group included Sir Tom O'Brien and Sir Harry Douglass (whom Cousins had supported for the chairmanship of the Economic Committee). Among the anti-Cousins faction were Sidney Greene, the railwaymen's leader, whose relations with Cousins had been strained ever since the London bus strike, and Harold (now Lord) Collison, the farm-workers' leader. At the next meeting, Ron Smith, of the Post Office Workers' Union, who had missed the first meeting, cast his vote in favour of Hayday, who was elected by four votes to three. These things might seem unimportant to the outsider, but within the narrow circle of trade union leaders such a defeat can be a considerable blow to a man's prestige.

A parallel incident had occurred at Berne in July 1960, when, at a Congress of the International Transport Workers'

F

Federation, there was a contest for a seat on the executive board between Cousins and Sidney Greene. In a secret ballot of the representatives of the thirty-six nations Greene defeated Cousins, who had been ITF President since 1958, by 2,100,000 votes to 1,787,000. Cousins had the humiliating experience of having to announce his own defeat from the chair. The railway unions backed Greene because they thought it was time the TGWU should give way to the railwaymen, and said that Arthur Deakin had only been installed as Britain's representative in the late 1940s to keep out the fellow-travelling Jim Figgins, the then NUR secretary. This row might seem utterly unimportant, but it soured relations between Cousins and the rail unions' leaders for a long time. The incident throws a not altogether creditable light on international trade union brotherhood. Two years later Cousins was re-elected President.

Cousins found things easier after George Woodcock succeeded Sir Vincent Tewson in 1960 as General Secretary of the TUC. It would be an understatement to say that neither Cousins nor Woodcock had 'got on' with Sir Vincent. It would equally be an over-statement to say that a Woodcock-Cousins 'axis' emerged, though the two men saw eye-to-eye to a remarkable degree on a number of industrial and trade union issues. They liked each other and at international conferences, preferred to spend an evening in each other's company rather than remain with the rest of the TUC party. Woodcock thought it stupid and unwise to try to isolate Cousins, or goad him, as some of the more waspish members of the General Council were prone to do.

Despite their very different backgrounds, the lorry driver who left school at fourteen and the Oxford-educated office administrator have the same basic conception about trade unionism and the same pragmatic approach to problems. Perhaps their biggest differences have arisen over politics. Cousins always took a violently pro-Labour line, while

Woodcock wanted to see the TUC becoming more a-political, and would no doubt echo Citrine's statement in 1938 that the TUC's 'conduct in dealing with any Government must be regulated by industrial and not political considerations'. Woodcock was not at all happy when first Hugh Gaitskell in 1959, and later Harold Wilson in 1964, used the Trade Union Congress platform as a launching-pad for their General Election campaigns.

When Cousins returned to the TUC fold in 1966, after twenty months' absence, George Woodcock's reaction was typical. 'I shall be glad to see Frank back,' he said. 'He is a nice lad to argue with.' Not all the members of the General Council shared Woodcock's enthusiasm. Some of them had got rather bored with what seemed to them interminable and often academic arguments between the two. 'They seem to indulge in a perpetual game of one-upmanship,' a union leader commented. Yet even the most right-wing members of the General Council were compelled to admit that Cousins was a valuable colleague. He was at his best in committee where he talked to the point; he could be relied upon to do his homework, and study his briefs.

Modern trade unions are practically a fifth estate of the realm, and there is hardly any aspect of public life and activity on which they do not have a say. A TUC leader has to shoulder a tremendous workload. Quite apart from running his own union and leading its negotiations, he has to serve on TUC committees and on the countless advisory and consultative bodies which governments set up to make sure that the workers' interests are represented. Cousins conscientiously played his full part in all these activities. Just as when he first became an organiser for his union, he set out to be the 'best' official in the business, so he determined to be one of the 'best' members of the General Council.

Cabinet Ministers have not always taken the TUC as seriously as it does itself. When Iain Macleod was Minister of Labour a deputation from the TUC came to see him and he was rather off-hand, where his predecessor Sir Walter (later Lord) Monckton would have soothed them. I remember asking Macleod why he had been so brusque. 'My dear girl, you don't expect me to go down on my knees and bow three times just because the TUC comes to see me,' was his reply.

8

More pay for more production

Iᴛ is now time to look at Cousins against a rather wider canvas, and to outline his views on some of the critical industrial issues of the mid-twentieth century. In many respects, he has been ahead of his critics. He has always held advanced ideas on industrial organisation and the application of technological discoveries. There is nothing of the 'Luddite' in his make-up.

The gospel according to Frank Cousins has always been 'More pay for more production'. In his view, 'Wage increases that result from rising output are the workers' share of the extra wealth they are helping to create'. In this attitude he has followed the Bevin tradition. When he was Minister of Labour during the war Bevin refused to listen to arguments that workers' earnings ought to be limited, and maintained that high wages were not necessarily inflationary if they led to higher production. 'The world won't come to an end because a worker earns more than £5 a week,' he used to say.

I recall two early occasions when Cousins' modern outlook amazed his audiences, who were expecting a left-wing firebrand. The first was at a British Productivity Council conference in May 1956 to launch a pamphlet on productivity in freight-handling. Cousins declared his full acceptance of the need for mechanical handling, but insisted that managements should take their workers into their confidence before introducing new machines and methods. This has been his constant theme.

A few months later, in October, he was a guest of honour

at the Institute of Directors' annual meeting at the London Festival Hall. His appearance on this apparently incongruous platform, so soon after his speech at the Brighton TUC, brought many businessmen to the verge of apoplexy and caused Lord Bracken to walk out. Cousins soon dispelled their fears:

> There seems to be a general idea that the wild men are taking over at Transport House and that the Davy Crockett hat is replacing the Homburg as a symbol of leadership. It isn't a true picture. We in the trade union movement are not entering a recklessly militant period of industrial relations. I believe that a most fruitful period lies ahead, in which we shall see a great development and diversification of good relations between employers and employed.

He added, however: 'This doesn't mean that we are going soft on wages,' and warned that the workers demanded the right to be *equal* partners in industry.

Cousins has always stipulated two main conditions for the workers' co-operation in increasing productivity:

1. They must be fully consulted about any changes affecting their wages and conditions, and their jobs, and

2. They must progressively share in the benefits of increased production.

Long before Ray Gunter introduced his Redundancy Act, Cousins was campaigning for adequate compensation for workers who were displaced by technological change. In 1959 he told his members they could not 'hide their heads in the sand of slogans and say "We won't accept redundancy",' and he went on: 'Unless you agree that men must go to new places or change their jobs, you cannot pretend you want a planned industry.'

This was in direct contrast to the Canute-like policy then adopted by the AEU National Committee, which had opposed redundancy *tout court*. Cousins' line was: 'Work for proper consultation and proper compensation—don't argue that the solution is for men to stay in the same jobs all the time and "share the misery".'

He has been far-sighted in his views on industrial training and technical education. He has campaigned persistently for more educational opportunities for young workers and for training, not only in craftsmanship, but in the wide range of semi-skilled work. In 1963 he told a union regional conference:

> We want real industrial training. We represent more skilled workers than many other organisations. Men should be paid adequately while they are being trained. We want mobility which can only come if there is adequate training.

The TGWU has often called for an end of the present narrow apprenticeship system and, as long ago as 1961, urged the need for a levy on employers to finance industry-wide training. This anticipated the Industrial Training Act of 1964, which was introduced by a Conservative Government and expanded by Labour when it came to power.

Cousins' own views on industrial training were set out in a speech in September 1964:

> So far, Britain has tried to approach the modern technical world with training and apprenticeship schemes related to a different age. Industrial training now is often unrealistic, quite unfair, and in many cases non-existent.

This theme has been pressed by his union on every possible occasion. Jack Jones, Assistant Executive Secretary and Cousins' close ally, told a conference of personnel officers in the spring of 1967 that, while the Industrial Training Boards had done a good job, 'we have yet to make the real breakthrough in industrial training away from the old apprenticeship pattern'. In his reckoning it would require something like a quarter of a million workers in Government training centres, or twenty times the present number, to catch up with the needs.

Long before many British union leaders recognised that the problem even existed Cousins accepted the inevitability of automation. His constant message to the workers has been on these lines:

> There is no need to fear automation, because automation and technological progress should be designed, if we are intelligent, to benefit labour conditions and our lives.

One of his first statements on becoming Minister of Technology was to an assembly of industrialists in London: 'Don't be afraid of automation, but don't make the workers afraid of it either.' He told a London Labour party conference in January 1966:

> There is no more important task for the Labour Government than to ensure that we secure the benefits of automation, without bringing with it the misery and upheaval caused to so many by the first industrial revolution.

He was chosen in 1961 to represent the TUC on the Department of Scientific and Industrial Research, and this proved a valuable apprenticeship for his later job. Of his experience, he later said:

> I went on DSIR with a great deal of trepidation because it is a body in which scientists and chemists and technologists sit with us. It was thrilling, it was great to listen to these men talking about the possibilities. It was paralysing to see the limitation of opportunity that comes because the dead hand of monetary control comes over it.

Cousins' own views on the application of science and technology to industry were never more clearly set out than at the Labour party conference at Scarborough in 1963. This was the conference at which Harold Wilson took as his main theme the need 'to re-state Socialism in terms of the scientific revolution', and he found in Frank Cousins an enthusiastic ally. Cousins congratulated Wilson on choosing this theme, and said:

> What is science? To many people it is different things. It can be the basis of those little thriller stories that you can buy in science fiction; it can be the background in which the terrible weapons of destruction are created; it can be many other things. To me, it means this: it is a vision with its working clothes on, nothing more and nothing less.

As on every occasion, he took the opportunity to stress the social implications of the scientific revolution.

> Remember there is a vital factor. Frightened workers will not participate . . . We are not willing to be guided into a new world, where half of the people do not even get the benefits of this world. We want a new world where training and skill is done for the benefit of assisting any change into a new order.

To those who heard this passionate, almost visionary, declaration of faith, it came as no surprise when Cousins was made Minister of Technology. But there were many among his critics who discerned a discrepancy between Cousins' principles and his practice. Ernest Marples, the Conservative spokesman on technology, said that the leader of 'one of the most reactionary unions in the country' had no right to preach modernisation to the engineering industry. Peter Walker, Shadow Minister of Transport, once challenged Cousins to a public debate on the 'crippling restrictive practices' of which his union was the 'arch-practitioner'. Had he accepted this challenge, Cousins would no doubt have retorted that the blame for what he preferred to call 'defensive' practices, lay with managements which failed to modernise their industrial relations, and with a society which did not guarantee full employment. He did not defend these practices, but sought to explain them to an uncomprehending public. Thus, he said of demarcation disputes:

Men are not arguing about who bores the holes or pulls the string. They are arguing about who is going to be in work, and who is going to be unemployed.

There is a credit, as well as a debit, side to the picture. It is painfully true that certain sections of the Transport Union have shown little enthusiasm for change and innovation, whatever their leaders may have said.

There is considerable over-manning throughout the transport industry. The situation in the docks, which are a law unto themselves, is described in the next chapter. In passenger transport there has been resistance, particularly in London, to the introduction of one-man, 'pay as you enter' buses and there is usually trouble about the revision of schedules. The market porters, especially in Covent Garden and Smithfield, have built up a network of restrictive practices and traditions; operating a tightly closed shop, the union can control labour supply and impose its own rules, often with the threat of withdrawal of labour.

The classic case occurred at Smithfield in 1954, during the so-called 'Bummarees'' strike, when Spencer Tribe was the TGWU market organiser. Tribe, one of the nearest approaches to an American waterfront union leader that the British movement has known, was the undisputed boss of Smithfield. A butcher had brought an action in the Mayor's and City of London Court to establish his right to carry away his own purchases of meat, instead of having them loaded by one of the licensed market TGWU porters. The judgment went in favour of the butcher and against the market tenant who had refused to let him take the meat. The men, however, threatened to strike if the butcher carried out the judgment, and Spencer Tribe declared: 'He said he would, the judge said he could, we said he could not and he did not.' Another Smithfield rule debarred a driver or his mate from pulling the meat from the front to the tailboard of his van, and this created a new class of workers known as the 'puller-back'.

At Covent Garden market strictly defined demarcation rules between the pitchers, the staff men and the porters often produced long delays and added to the cost of fruit and vegetables.

Some of the worst time-wasting practices were stopped as a result of the reorganisation of both markets, and little has been heard about them in recent years. But there is no doubt that the activities of the men at Smithfield and Covent Garden helped to give the whole trade union movement the bad name it acquired during the 1950s.

A more recent example of resistance to change occurred in the autumn of 1965 when there was a dispute among the Longbridge car-delivery workers over a proposal by British Railways to convey new cars from the British Motor Corporation's plant direct by rail to the South of England. The drivers saw their jobs disappearing, and one of the union's Midlands officials declared:

> It might be in the national interest, but it is not in the interests of the union. We cannot have a railway train putting our members out of work.

He added that the dispute might have been avoided if there had been proper consultation with the Union beforehand.

Against such examples may be set the acceptance by the TGWU of British Railways' proposal to introduce freight-liner trains, at a time when the National Union of Railwaymen was boycotting the scheme. Even though this may not have been altogether disinterested, since the Union's lorry drivers stood to gain from this development, the decision was welcomed by the Government as a step towards improved efficiency.

It may also be said that the TGWU is by no means the worst offender and its record on restrictive practices compares favourably with that, say, of the newspaper printing unions.

On the credit side it is also salutary to remember that the Transport and General Workers' Union was a pioneer in negotiating the productivity agreements, which became the height of fashion in the mid-1960s. The textbook case, and the first of its kind, was the deal at Esso's oil refinery at Fawley, where the TGWU is the sole representative of the non-craft workers. It was concluded in 1960, after the long and patient negotiations described so admirably by Allan Flanders in his book on Fawley. In return for increased rates of pay the unions agreed to certain changes in their working practices which had militated against efficiency, and also to cuts in systematic overtime. The results were remarkable. Between 1960 and 1966 the labour force fell from 3,500 to 2,500. The agreement saved the company many thousands of pounds in labour costs. Without it, Esso would have had to engage another 300 men, in addition to the original 3,500. For the workers themselves, average hourly earnings increased by 35 per cent in the first two years after the signing of the agreement, compared with an 11–12 per cent rise in manufacturing industry generally. Ernest Allen, TGWU regional secretary in Southampton, who had been closely associated with the Fawley project, later described it as 'the most wonderful, exciting thing that has happened to me as a trade union official. I am a better man because I knew Fawley.'

Esso negotiated a parallel agreement with its 120 employees at the Milford Haven refinery and one for its distribution network, which was designed to increase the usage of road tankers from eleven to twenty hours a day. The other big oil companies, Shell, Mobil, and Regent, followed suit, and struck productivity bargains with their employees.

The sceptics suggested that oil, being a capital-intensive and wealthy industry, could well afford this type of agreement, but it would not be applicable elsewhere. They were proved wrong. Successful deals were negotiated in a wide variety of organisations, such as Rank Hovis McDougall,

British European Airways, British Oxygen Company and Morganite Carbon.

That with British Oxygen merits separate mention, because, as it was due to operate from August 1st, 1966, it fell victim to the wage freeze, and the Government declared the scheme illegal under the Prices and Incomes Act. The pact, which applied to some 4,200 workers at the company's fifty-five plants, took two years to negotiate and was designed 'to increase productivity without contributing to inflation'. It provided for a progressive cut, amounting to 15 per cent, in overtime, the introduction of new and more flexible working arrangements, and in return the workers received a bonus of 25 per cent on their weekly wage, improved status and numerous fringe benefits. As it turned out, it proved impracticable to 'unscramble' the agreement.

An important agreement was reached with Imperial Chemical Industries, with the twofold object of improving efficiency and enhancing the employees' status. An experiment was made at four sites, under which job grades were to be streamlined, an annual wage system introduced and changes made in existing practices. The national secretary of the TGWU chemicals' group described it as 'an enlightened attempt to deal with the challenge of modern industry'.

The various productivity agreements differ in scope and in detail, but all have the same fundamental purpose as the Fawley deal: higher pay for higher production. All include an element which can only be described as 'buying out the union rule book'.

The Transport Union embarked on its own campaign to encourage productivity. It set up a special production and research department in Transport House, under Ellen McCullough and included productivity training in its courses for shop stewards and officials.

Because of their initial enthusiasm, the union's leaders reacted all the more bitterly when a stop was imposed on further productivity bargaining after July 20th, 1966. The sense of anticlimax and disillusionment played no small part in their subsequent hostility to the Government's prices and incomes policy. Yet, the union's initiative was vindicated by the final report of the Prices and Incomes Board on productivity agreements. The Board had been asked in August 1966 to examine various agreements to see whether they were 'genuine', including those reached with Esso and British Oxygen. It gave a general blessing to productivity bargaining and, among its conclusions, found no evidence that it tended to push up wages, regardless of productivity, in other industries. The agreements, said the Board, had resulted in important savings; they had led to more effective control by management and given greater security to the workpeople.

9

The dockland jungle

S OON after he became General Secretary I remember
Cousins telling me that as a road haulage man he knew all
about the conditions of lorry drivers but was not very familiar
with those of the dockers—a surprisingly frank admission
from one who so often gave the impression of omniscience.
He rapidly sought to make good the omission and briefed
himself thoroughly on the problems of this key section of the
Union. At first, he told me, he had entertained some doubts
about a system in which union representatives served jointly
with employers on the National Dock Labour Board and
thereby assumed disciplinary functions over the members.
But after talking things over with Tim O'Leary, the national
docks' group secretary, and other officials, he came round to
accepting that there were certain advantages in the system,
although he consistently stressed that union members on
national or local dock boards should never forget that their
first loyalty must be to the Union.

The dock labour scheme, which was established in 1947
and was Bevin's brain-child, is peculiar to port transport. It
presented a sort of half-way house to the complete decasualisation which Bevin dreamed of, but nearly twenty years after
its introduction there was still only about a quarter of the
labour force in permanent employment in the 'Pool'.

The docks are the only industry in which workers' representatives share certain joint responsibilities with the employers. Many people expected that when the coal mines
were nationalised the miners' union would play a part in

running the industry. But from the start the National Union of Mineworkers refused to become directly associated with management, although it released some of its leaders to serve on the National Coal Board at various levels. The departure of men like Ebby Edwards and James Bowman to serve on the Board led to a serious weakening in the Union, and it was always rather galling for them to be identified in the men's eyes with the bosses' side. The railway unions adopted the same attitude when the railways were nationalised.

The experience of joint control in the docks has certainly not been very encouraging. Ever since the end of the war the docks, notably London, Liverpool and Hull, have been a trouble spot. Disputes between 1947 and 1955 cost the industry nearly 350,000 man-days—ten times as many as in the comparable pre-war period. The situation improved between 1960 and 1964, but out of 421 strikes during these four years, no fewer than 410, representing 94 per cent of the lost days, were unofficial. Since the Transport Union, which caters for about 85 per cent of the country's 65,000 dockers, did not declare any strikes official during this period, its rate must be reckoned as 100 per cent.

It is significant, perhaps, that less than half the strikes were about normal industrial issues, such as wages and piece-rates. Nearly a third were in protest against Dock Board decisions or discipline, and about a quarter were due to inter-union troubles.

There is clearly something very rotten in the state of dock-land and it is perhaps necessary to look briefly at the causes of the labour unrest, and the reasons for the failure of the Transport Union to prevent its authority being usurped by unofficial elements.

Since 1946 there have been countless surveys and enquiries, culminating in the authoritative committee of enquiry, headed by Lord Devlin, in 1965. All agreed that the underlying cause of the trouble was the casual nature of employment and that the only possible cure was genuine decasualisation. The Devlin Committee offered a productivity package deal—decasualisation, with engagement of all port workers on a weekly basis, in return for the ending of restrictive practices and the acceptance of modernisation and mechanisation. 'Casual labour produces a casual attitude,' commented the Devlin Report, drawing attention to the excessive number of casual employers who 'are a cause of both inefficiency and dissension'. Most of these failed to provide even elementary welfare facilities and the standard of amenities has been far below the acceptable standard of modern industry. The London Communist party was not exaggerating when in evidence to the Devlin Committee it stated:

> Canteen facilities are so decrepit and outdated that dockers have the choice of going outside the dock or joining long queues for unsatisfactory food in dirty surroundings; men refuse to use toilets that are uncleaned and not looked after . . . baths or showers are conspicuous by their absence; each year one docker in every eight suffers a serious injury and one in every 1,500 is killed at work.

Cousins himself one day paid a visit to a docks welfare centre and inspected the canteen. He was shocked and amazed. 'Disgusting!' he exclaimed. 'I wouldn't bring my dog to eat here.'

The docks are a world of their own, with their own mystique and traditions. Until fairly recently, before dispersal and re-housing, the dockers formed a community in London almost as isolated as the miners' communities in the Welsh valleys. They have an overwhelming sense of solidarity and react instinctively and explosively if there is even a rumour that one of their mates is being treated unjustly. The Leggett Report in 1951 put it vividly:

> It appears to be incredibly easy to bring dock workers out on strike. We were given repeated instances of men stopping work almost automatically, with little or no idea

G

why they were stopping. In the words of one witness, himself a dock worker, 'All that was needed was for a man to go round the docks shouting "All out" and waving the men off the ships and out they would come'.

This sense of loyalty does not explain, or excuse, the failure of the Transport and General Workers' Union to control its dockland members, or to snatch the initiative from the unofficial leaders. One of the first acts of these unofficial leaders is usually to appoint a public relations officer. I have often been called to 'briefing' meetings with the strike PRO in some obscure Whitechapel pub or 'caff', at a time when it was almost impossible to obtain any information from the union officials. One of the big London strikes in the late 1940s was only called off after Mr Attlee, then Prime Minister, broadcast an appeal to the dockers over the heads of the union leaders. (It was actually Ernie Bevin who wrote his script.) Under Communist leadership in London, and the Trotskyites in Liverpool, the unofficial elements always seem to have set the pace.

The situation has been bedevilled by inter-union rivalry. The Stevedores and Dockers' union, commonly known as the 'Blue Union', developed during the late forties as a result of dissatisfaction with the TGWU. Its main strength has been in London, Liverpool and Hull, but nobody knows for sure how many members it has.

Transport Union officials deny that they are out of touch with the men, and point out that they have more officers in proportion to their members in the docks than in any other section. Many officials earn far less than the men they represent; they have an arduous job, involving a great deal of travelling and complicated negotiations on piece rates. Most are conscientious and hard-working, but, as the Devlin Report noted, some of them tend to take a rather defeatist 'nothing to be done about it' attitude. The Devlin Report said: 'If the present officers were conscious of working for an organisation which commanded the loyalty, affection and support of the great majority of dockers, it might be easier for them to feel they were doing a worthwhile and competent job.'

The first serious attempts from within the industry itself to put its own house in order were made in 1961, after two major and crippling strikes in the Port of London. Mr (later Sir) Andrew Crichton, the then Chairman of the National Port Employers' Association and co-chairman with Frank Cousins of the industry's National Joint Council, got in touch with Cousins at Transport House. 'Frank, if *we* don't do something at once the country will be absolutely fed up with us,' he said. Crichton and his number two, Maurice Gifford, went to the Union's headquarters and had a long talk with Cousins and Tim O'Leary.

The four men met continuously to thrash things out and drew up what became known in dock circles as the 'Cousins/Crichton Manifesto' or 'New Testament' and to the wider public as the 'National Directive'. This provided that, in return for the introduction of a weekly employment basis and the reaffirmation of the dock labour scheme, the dockers would work for the elimination of restrictive practices and accept labour mobility and mechanisation. It was a forward-looking document, and bore the imprint of Frank Cousins. 'He put in a terrific amount of work and was exceedingly good at drafting,' commented Sir Andrew Crichton six years later. 'He came to life over this, and in my view he really shone.'

Largely as a result of their co-operation in producing this manifesto, the two men forged a close alliance, based on mutual liking and respect. They had had their differences. At one meeting of the Joint Ports Council, during the Selwyn Lloyd period of wage restraint, the employers' side said 'No' to a union wage claim. Cousins, who on this occasion had taken over the chair from O'Leary who usually presided for the workers, accused the employers of being the tools of the

Tory Government. Crichton exploded. 'How dare you say that?' he asked. 'You know perfectly well that we are an independent body, and we take orders from nobody.' He demanded an immediate retraction.

The atmosphere in the Council chamber was electric. Cousins, who was not used to being talked to like that, blenched and for a moment it seemed that he, too, might explode. But he mumbled an apology and no more was said. From that moment he and Crichton became firm friends.

The two Chairmen 'sold' the document to their joint Council which in October 1961 issued a decasualisation directive down the line to all joint port committees calling, optimistically, for action by New Year 1962.

The Directive was the forerunner of the productivity agreements which became so fashionable during the 1960s. The Rochdale Committee on the Ports in 1962 described it as 'a document of first-class importance'. The Devlin Committee accepted it as 'the best line of approach to the reform of industrial relations in the docks' and incorporated its seven principles into its own recommendations.

Yet the Directive remained a dead letter. Why? Devlin wanted to know when he conducted his own enquiry. He blamed the port employers for their failure to reorganise their structure and shed some of the 'dead weight of casual employers', and the unions for failing to prepare their members for change. The Transport Union had accepted the Directive, but had made no positive contribution to working it out. 'There have now been four years during which the T and G might have been putting new ideas across to its members and by so doing, re-establishing themselves as a force in the docks. There is need for action now, and by now we mean today,' Devlin thundered. That was in August 1965.

Frank Cousins, as General Secretary of the Transport Union and leader of 85 per cent of the nation's dockers, must bear his share of responsibility for those four wasted years. Both his friends and his critics agree that he did not spend enough time seeing things at first-hand, but leaned very heavily on the advice of his permanent officials. In this, after all, he was following the correct constitutional practice of the Union, which is so compartmentalised that officials of particular sections tend to resent any interference.

Jack Dash, the leader of the unofficial element in the Port of London, told me: 'Cousins is the finest General Secretary I have served under, but he ought to come down to the docks more often and see for himself. He relies too much on his officials.' I doubt very much whether Dash would welcome evidence of a stronger grip at the centre, since his own strength has lain in his ability to persuade the dockers that he is the best custodian of their interests.

Of Jack Dash and his unofficial Liaison Committee, the Devlin Committee said: 'In London the unofficial leadership is strong enough to amount to a rival power. No strong union can allow unofficial leadership to prevail in the way in which it has prevailed in London.'

Dash himself is a colourful Cockney, and a lifelong member of the Communist party. A slightly built, wiry man, now in his sixties, he works, usually stripped to the waist, alongside 'the boys' in the Royal Docks, and belongs to Branch 1137, universally known, he claims, as 'the branch with the punch'. He lives in a modern apartment, furnished in Scandinavian style, on the sixteenth floor of an LCC skyscraper housing estate in Stepney—'near the London Opera Centre, you can't miss it', he told me when I arranged to call on him. As well as being an agitator, he is something of a scholar and a painter, and is much sought after by university debating societies. He is rarely out of the public eye, much to the chagrin of union officials.

Dash claims that his committee, which is elected at dock-gate meetings, is more in touch with rank-and-file opinion than official branch meetings, which are usually poorly attended. He sees it as a ginger group, acting within the Union, not seeking to usurp its functions, but just pushing it along the desired lines. He can exert a magnetic hold over the dockers, even if they don't agree with his extremist views. 'We don't listen to 90 per cent of what he says, but we need him. He keeps the employers on their toes,' was a typical docker comment. Very few dockers are Communist, but they like militant leadership and suspect that some of their union officials are hand in glove with the employers, with whom they sit on the Dock Board. They would rather have the snap show of hands decision at a dock-gate meeting than wait for the cumbersome working of the constitutional machinery.

From his Stepney eyrie, Dash draws up periodical broadsheets and leaflets, calling for militant action. Here is a typical example illustrating a campaign against redundancy:

ATTENTION ALL PORT WORKERS! ! ! ! ! ! ! !
        DONT BE CONNED! ! ! ! ! ! ! !
URGENT! ! ! ! !   URGENT! ! ! ! !   URGENT! ! ! ! !
WE SAY:
DEMAND IMMEDIATE REMOVAL OF ALL
    REDUNDANCY CLAUSES! ! ! !
NOT ONE MAN OFF! ! !
TO YOUR BRANCHES—DEMAND ACTION
YOUR JOB IS THREATENED
                                        Jackie Dash
                                        Liaison Committee

This sort of propaganda, with its liberal use of exclamation marks, may seem naive in a world conditioned to the soft-sell methods of public relations officers, but it is only one weapon in the Dash armoury. The Devlin Report noted: 'Mr Dash holds frequent dock-gate meetings with a loud-speaker van. The T and G only occasionally replies in kind.'

Despite the strictures on their leadership, Transport Union officials welcomed the Devlin Report. Cousins himself was in the Government when the Report came out, but its theme was very much in accordance with the National Directive of 1961 which he and Crichton had pioneered. Harry Nicholas, acting General Secretary, issued a statement, within a few hours of the Report's publication:

> At long last the dreams of our forefathers on dockland are likely to be achieved and the status of the dock worker properly recognised.

A broadsheet was circulated, explaining Devlin to the dockers. (According to Dash, this broadsheet plus two dock-gate meetings represented the sum total of the official campaign to 'put over' Devlin. Union dock officials, however, say this is a distortion and that they in fact mounted a major campaign in the ports.)

The irrepressible Jackie Dash and his Liaison Committee took a very different view of Devlin. While they welcomed some aspects of the Report, they warned that 'it could be the basis for a major attack on manning scales, protective practices, working hours and conditions' and would increase the employers' hold over the men.

The Devlin Report had condemned practices of bad time-keeping, such as late starting, early finishing and lengthy tea-breaks, and had criticised the 'continuity rule', under which a man is entitled to finish a job which he has begun. According to the Report: 'The rule is wasteful in terms of money, time and efficiency. Even in its mildest form, it prevents transfer of labour from ship to ship or from ship to quay.' Dash hit back in his Bulletin:

> Our so-called 'restrictive' practices are brought about by a desire to protect our jobs, our health and on some occasions our lives. . . . The continuity rule is priceless, no consideration will induce us to part with it.

Negotiations on the basic rates dragged on, and the Devlin Committee was called upon to sort things out. In October 1966 it recommended a basic weekly wage of £11 1s 8d plus £2 for modernisation, with a guaranteed minimum of £15. These proposals were accepted by fifty-seven votes to twenty-four at a docker's delegate conference at Transport House in December 1966. Tim O'Leary hailed this as 'the start of a new era'.

After this conference there were some signs that the influence of the unofficial Liaison Committee was starting to wane. The credit squeeze caused considerable unemployment in the docks, and unemployment is never conducive to militancy. When Jack Dash called a token strike in May 1967, over a pay demand, it proved a complete flop. Only about one in ten of London's dockers responded and the strike was virtually limited to his home ground in the Royal group of docks.

Tim O'Leary's 'new era' was slow in making its appearance. Despite pressure from the National Modernisation Committee set up to give effect to the Devlin recommendations, negotiations on pay and productivity dragged on. There were delays on both sides, and tough bargaining took place at every port about the ending of restrictive practices. A 'chicken and egg' situation developed. The dockers said: No concessions without full decasualisation, while the employers insisted on concrete evidence that the men would first accept modernisation and end their restrictive practices.

The delays were particularly frustrating to the Minister of Labour, who had originally whipped both sides into activity. In August he issued an Order setting September 18th, 1967, as the deadline for decasualisation. But though the employers had by then reduced their numbers from 1,500 to about 350, the issues of pay and redundancy were still unresolved. An unofficial stoppage flared up on Merseyside, which led

The Times to comment: 'Once again it demonstrates the apparent inability of the Union to control its dockworker members.'

This Merseyside dispute developed into a major stoppage, involving about 9,000 dockers. Meanwhile in London Jack Dash reasserted his sway and succeeded in bringing out, and keeping out, between 5,000 and 6,000 men.

When the situation began to get out of hand, Cousins cut short a visit to Mexico, but he was no more able than any of his officials to get the strikers back, despite a personal appeal to Dash and a promise that the Union would take up the men's grievances. He joined with George Woodcock in rejecting the Minister of Labour's theory of a 'Red Plot' and adopted a very un-Deakinish attitude towards the strikers:

> I am not prepared to lambast the Liverpool dockers when we know grievances exist. They feel they have grievances and we know that some of them are real ones. They may be misguided in their methods . . . It is our responsibility to help them solve their problems.

The dockers' strikes cost altogether half a million working days and inflicted untold damage on Britain's trade. They were, indeed, mentioned by the Prime Minister on November 19th as among the factors which had contributed to devaluation.

Cousins was severely criticised for his failure to re-establish union authority. Thus the President of the Chamber of Shipping, Mr Anthony Cayzer, declared angrily: 'It is time that Mr Cousins did his job. So far he has been conspicuous by his strange silence and lack of leadership in the docks.'

Cousins may have been on the side-lines during the interminable talks about the Devlin Report, but there is evidence that he was becoming increasingly disturbed about modernisation of the docks. In the spring of 1967 he visited Millwall docks to see a highly sophisticated method of cargo-handling on the new Fred Olsen line ship *Black Prince*, and told the owners:

> What the Union is striving for is a good and realistic living for the dockers, the best that can be obtained, and it might be that developments of this sort will make the realisation of this objective earlier than many people thought possible.

Early in May he called on his old friend Sir Andrew Crichton, who had become head of a shipping consortium for developing container handling. They lunched together in a quiet room at the Great Eastern Hotel and Cousins expressed his concern about the effects on the dock labour force of 'containerisation'. How could the run-down of the numbers employed be effected with the least possible hardship to the men? Could it be done by introducing an earlier retirement age? How could the changes be put over to the men? These were some of the points they discussed over lunch. Cousins left almost immediately on a visit to the USA, but promised that the all-efficient Jack Jones would keep an eye on things in his absence.

Many varying estimates have been made about the effects of the 'container revolution'. One estimate is that, over the next decade, only about 40,000 dockers (20,000 fewer than in 1967) will be required to handle Britain's port traffic. At his own union conference in July Cousins rejected as 'wildly exaggerated' a report that 90 per cent of dock labour would eventually not be required, although he did not minimise the threat to dockers' jobs and insisted on the need for proper redundancy arrangements. At this conference he stressed that decasualisation was only the first step on the road to full nationalisation of the nation's ports.

10

'No compromise with evil'

THE 'Ban the Bomb' movement swept across Britain like
a prairie fire during the late 1950s. Not since the Spanish
Civil War had any 'Cause' so dramatically captured the
imagination of the young, or rallied so many varied sections
of opinion under a single umbrella. The Campaign for
Nuclear Disarmament, itself an agglomeration of pacifist,
Quaker, intellectual, non-political, socialist, liberal, progressive and skiffle groups, was born on January 15th, 1958,
in Canon John Collins' study at Number 2 Amen Court,
hard by St Paul's. Its original executive committee reads
rather like a blurb for a *New Statesman* editorial, and its
first list of sponsors was heavily biassed towards the Arts,
rather than politics or the trade unions.

The CND was formally launched, six weeks later, at a
crowded meeting in the Central Hall, Westminster. It there
established itself as a unilateralist movement, calling on
Britain 'to renounce unconditionally the use or production of
nuclear weapons'. The organisers decided to join with an
existing anti-nuclear group, which later became the Direct
Action Committee, in sponsoring the Easter march from
London to Aldermaston.

The Direct Action group contained Quakers, pacifists and
anarchists, and, in its own words, was 'not primarily interested in the return of any political party at the next election'.
Canon Collins and his committee reckoned it would be
wiser to have this group inside, rather than on the fringe,
even though the association with such extremist elements

might (and in the event did) lose the CND some of its more 'respectable' supporters. But he, and most CND leaders, agreed with Kingsley Martin that they should concentrate on converting the Labour party. Martin wrote:

> Unless they work through the Labour movement, nuclear disarmers are simply marching about to satisfy their own consciences and expressing their sense of the sin and horror of nuclear war.

The first march, despite bitterly cold and wet weather, succeeded beyond the wildest dreams of its sponsors, and was joined by between 5,000 and 10,000 people. Frank Cousins and his wife Nance did not take part in the 1958 march, but the following year, when the marchers reversed direction and came from Aldermaston to London, he and his family were 'espied' in the crowd that thronged Trafalgar Square. (Quite an achievement to pick out a single individual from a crowd of about 20,000!) From the plinth of Nelson's column Canon Collins boomed down the loudspeaker: 'Stand up and be counted.' But Cousins declined to join the platform party, even though it included his fellow trade union leader Bob Willis, who was that year's chairman of the TUC.

The next year, and for at least two subsequent years, Cousins joined the march at Turnham Green on the Easter Monday, and walked beside Canon Collins at the head of the long procession that snaked its way through the London streets to Trafalgar Square. Canon Collins has recalled to me how Cousins expressed delight at the large numbers of young people on the march, and regret that the Labour party seemed incapable of inspiring the same enthusiasm. Cousins made this point when he spoke in the Square in 1960.

'Let us forget Clause Four and concentrate on nuclear disarmament,' he said. That was the only way in which the party could become an inspiration to progressive and idealistic youth. 'My organisation has been proud to be in the front of the protest to get rid of these weapons.'

Although he was publicly identified with the Aldermaston march, Cousins never became prominent in the counsels of the CND, or joined its executive—the Campaign never took on individual members. He had a rooted dislike and fear of being 'used' by any organisation. Nevertheless his accession to their ranks was a major feather in the CND cap, and its leaders were able at least on one occasion to use his good offices in a practical way.

In the autumn of 1960, when the tidal wave of unilateralism looked like engulfing the Labour party conference, a sudden snag developed. Lord Russell, the CND President, told Canon Collins that he proposed making a speech in Trafalgar Square on September 24th in support of direct action. The CND executive was horrified, and Canon Collins suggested that it might be helpful if Frank Cousins were asked to tell Lord Russell what sort of effect such a declaration would have on the party conference. Cousins agreed to do so, and told Lord Russell that this would be 'most unhelpful'. Lord Russell agreed to postpone his statement, but not apparently his plans. The news of the formation of the Committee of 100, pledged to civil disobedience, broke in the London *Evening Standard*, and an irreconcilable split developed between him and Canon Collins. Lord Russell resigned from the CND and became President of the Committee of 100 on October 22nd. By then the Labour party vote was in the bag, but the sit-down Gandhi tactics of Russell and his followers undoubtedly tarnished the whole of the unilateralists' image. It contributed to the reversal of the Labour party's vote in 1961 and the eventual decline of the CND as a force in politics.

We must now look a little more closely at Frank Cousins' own position vis-à-vis the CND, and the interminable arguments about the Bomb within the Labour movement.

The events of the Brighton conference of 1957 have been described in an earlier chapter and another context (see p. 32). It is significant that long before the birth of the CND Cousins had nailed his colours to the mast, and publicly declared his opposition to nuclear weapons. It is worth recording his words at Brighton (since they were so often to be repeated almost verbatim):

> I am not regarded in trade union circles as an emotional man, but on this thing I am proud to be emotional. I have a six-year-old daughter and I will not compromise with anybody on the future of that child.

Calling on the British Labour movement to 'take the moral lead', he went on:

> We must say that this nation, of all nations, great or small, however we may like to think of ourselves, does not approve of the maintenance and manufacture, either by ourselves or anyone else, of this idiot's weapon. *There is no compromise with evil.*

Aneurin Bevan, replying for the National Executive Committee, called for the rejection of unilateralism. 'If you carry this resolution and follow out all its implications, you will send a British Foreign Secretary, whoever he may be, naked into the conference chamber.' This famous phrase, actually borrowed from the Durham miners' leader, Sam Watson, made a deep impression on the delegates. Only 781,000 votes were cast in favour of the unilateralist resolution, compared with 5,836,000 votes (including that of the TGWU) against. The triumph of the platform seemed complete and at that stage CND was a cloud on the horizon no bigger than a man's hand.

The vote at the Brighton conference marked the end of the Bevanites as an organised force. Without the man who had given his name, unwittingly if not unwillingly, to the group, the rebels were left leaderless and fragmented. Attempts to revive the moribund 'Victory for Socialism' group made little headway and attracted the support of no more than about forty MPs. Even at that early stage there was speculation about whether Cousins could be persuaded to throw in his lot with the political left and fill the gap created by Bevan's departure. Cousins himself never showed the slightest desire to do so, and indeed took every opportunity to deny any such ambition.

Despite their sweeping majority at Brighton, the official leadership began to take serious note of the threat on their left flank from the mushrooming unilateralist movement. Expecting an early general election, the National Executive took steps to close the ranks. It set up a joint committee with the TUC in the spring of 1958 to draw up a new defence policy statement. This committee was dominated by right-wingers, but it contained at least two potential rebels— Cousins from the TUC side and Tom Driberg, representing the NEC. The committee worked out a statement calling among other things, for an end of British thermo-nuclear tests and delays in establishing missile bases in East Anglia. Driberg described this statement as 'an agreed practical basis upon which we all of us can unite'. Cousins, likewise, appears to have accepted it. At any rate he did not take part in the international debates, either at the TUC or the party conference that year. At both conferences motions for unilateral disarmament were heavily defeated.

In 1959 the tide again turned towards the unilateralists. Cousins was becoming increasingly intractable. He joined with Bob Willis in refusing to sign a policy statement which did not go far enough in dissociating Britain from nuclear weapons, and he did not warm to Gaitskell's idea of a non-nuclear club. At his own union conference in the Isle of Man that summer a seven-point resolution, which was patently unilateralist, was adopted by an overwhelming majority.

Cousins himself argued that there was nothing in the

TGWU resolution which conflicted with official policy, but Gaitskell put a different interpretation on it. That same weekend he hit back at the unilateralists in a speech at Workington:

> Our party decisions are not dictated by one man whether he be the Leader of the party, our spokesman on foreign affairs, or the General Secretary of the Transport and General Workers' Union. It is not right that a future Labour Government should be committed by conference decisions on every matter of detail for all time.

Cousins carried his own conference with him, but he failed to swing over the Trades Union Congress. The General Council, meeting on the eve of the 1959 Blackpool conference, decided by twenty-eight votes to five to oppose the TGWU resolution. Some of his delegation urged Cousins to withdraw it, because of the damage the split was doing to the party's election prospects. He refused, and was even more outspoken than he had been in 1957:

> I say for the Transport and General Workers' Union and I say as a father, that I cannot and will not see a situation where I would be a party to using this weapon against anyone.

The TGWU resolution was defeated by a two to one majority. A remarkable somersault by the National Union of General and Municipal Workers helped to swell the support for the official policy. This traditionally loyalist union had, at its June conference, accidentally gone unilateralist. (It was said that the multilateralists were out having a tea-break when the vote was taken.) Sir Thomas Williamson, its General Secretary, decided to recall the delegates in August to reconsider their attitude in the light of the latest official policy statement. The earlier decision was handsomely reversed. It may have been doubtful democracy, but it saved Gaitskell and his policy.

No Labour party conference was held that autumn because of the general election. The much-publicised and deepening fissure over defence undoubtedly contributed to the Labour party's defeat in 1959.

The unilateralist movement reached its peak in 1960. Roy Jenkins wrote in an essay on Hugh Gaitskell (published shortly after his death):

> During the spring and summer of 1960, the unilateralist forces built up with frightening speed. Union after union toppled almost casually into their camp. Gaitskell's position became more exposed than that of any party leader since Baldwin in 1938.

The first unions to topple were the Distributive Workers and the Amalgamated Engineering Union, both of which went unilateralist at their Easter conferences. The 1960 Aldermaston march was, for its organisers, the biggest and best they had held, and it seemed there was no stopping the CND snowball.

As early as March, Cousins had taken the initiative in suggesting that the TUC should hold fresh defence talks with the Labour party. Sir Vincent Tewson consulted with Gaitskell but they decided, astonishingly enough, that there was no immediate urgency. It was not until after the Easter conferences that the 'urgency' was discovered, and even then a joint meeting was not arranged until May 31st.

A joint drafting committee, with four from each side and again including Cousins and Driberg, was formed and met almost non-stop to try to thrash out a new formula. George Brown and Dick Crossman played a prominent part in the drafting, and by June seemed to be on the verge of an acceptable agreement. Hugh Gaitskell, who was in an uncompromising mood—he had already decided to retreat over the public ownership Clause Four in order to concentrate on defence—sat in on the final session and amended the Brown-Crossman draft to a point where Crossman threatened to

H

walk out. The two peace-makers, who were trying to bridge
the gap, found their efforts at mediation nullified. Cousins
later admitted that he found the situation acutely embarrass-
ing.

The TUC was held at the Isle of Man, scene of Cousins'
earlier triumph. The TGWU resolution, on the same lines as
its 1959 resolution, rejected the idea of any defence policy
based on nuclear weapons or the threat of their use. It was
carried by a sizable majority (4,356,000 to 3,213,000). The
AEU, with the lack of logic which so often seems to charac-
terise trade union thinking, supported both the TGWU
resolution and the official defence policy, and thus committed
the great British trade union movement to facing both ways.
The official statement was carried by 690,000 votes.

The stage was thus set for the Scarborough showdown.
Given Gaitskell's inflexibility, the failure of the Brown-
Crossman peace-making efforts and the sheer force of trade
union arithmetic, the clash and its results were inevitable.

My colleague Roy Nash, then on the *News Chronicle*, and I
wandered into the lounge of the Royal Hotel, headquarters
of the NEC, on the Saturday evening. The atmosphere was
icy. The three-piece band may have drowned the conversation but it did not produce any conviviality. The Gaitskells
and their friends were sipping coffee in one corner of the
room. At the far end a group of left-wingers, including the
Dribergs and Michael Foot, were joined by Cousins and his
wife and later by Canon Collins. It was the Morecambe
'divide' all over again. At that ill-starred conference in 1952,
to be seen by Herbert Morrison talking to Nye Bevan was to
be immediately dubbed a 'traitor', and vice versa. The lot of
a reporter, seeking only a story, was not a happy one, either
in 1952 or in 1960.

On the Sunday afternoon the CND held a mammoth rally.
A long procession marched round the Royal Hotel, where the
National Executive was in session, waving their banners and

shouting slogans: 'Down with the Bomb' and 'Gaitskell must go'.

The climax came on Wednesday morning, October 5th, in the Spa Grand Hall, which was packed almost to suffocation. Cousins strode to the rostrum to move his by now familiar resolution. This time there were six points:

1. A complete rejection of any defence policy based on the threat of the use of strategic or tactical nuclear weapons;

2. The permanent cessation of the manufacture or testing of nuclear and thermo-nuclear weapons;

3. The cessation of aircraft patrols carrying nuclear weapons from British bases;

4. Continued opposition to missile bases in Britain.

Points 5 and 6, unexceptionably, called for strengthening of the United Nations, with the admission of China, and for the reopening of talks leading to a general disarmament convention.

Cousins pinpointed the division between this policy and that of the NEC as being 'one simple issue of difference'.

> The NEC believes that the policies of the Western alliance and our own country ought to be based on the theory of having the Bomb; we think they ought to be based on the opposite theory of not having the Bomb.

The debate that followed was long and passionate, serious and sombre, and lasted till mid-afternoon. Then Gaitskell rose to wind up. He made what many regarded as the finest speech of his political career, but others took as a declaration of war. Remarking that he could not understand the precise meaning of some parts of the resolution, he challenged Cousins to say exactly what he meant. Did he mean that NATO should give up its nuclear weapons? Or that Britain should get out of NATO and withdraw from the Western alliance? Some organisations, he said, which had withdrawn their resolutions in favour of the TGWU, had made it clear that this was what they wanted, but Cousins had not said where he stood.

Noting rather bitterly that the issue had probably already been determined by union decisions, taken even before the NEC policy statement was available, he affirmed that the vast majority of Labour MPs were opposed to neutralism and would certainly refuse to accept the dictates of the conference.

> What sort of people do you think we are? Do you think we can simply accept a decision of this kind? Do you think that we can become overnight the pacifists, unilateralists and fellow-travellers that other people are?

Cousins was not the only member of the audience who resented the implication that to be against the Bomb was to be a fellow traveller. It was, indeed, a peculiar lapse on Gaitskell's part, comparable with his speech at Stalybridge after the Morecambe conference, when he alleged that about one-sixth of the constituency party delegates were Communist or Communist-inspired. This estimate, it later transpired, was based on a conversation with Ian Mackay of the *News Chronicle*, whose bent for the picturesque was at times stronger than his arithmetic.

In the full glare of the TV lights Gaitskell, who was wearing dark glasses, paused for a glass of water, mopped his brow and then came to his peroration with a final appeal to delegates to reject the 'suicidal path' of unilateral disarmament:

> We may lose the vote today and the result may deal this Party a grave blow. . . . There are some of us, Mr Chairman, who will fight and fight and fight again to save the Party we love. We will fight and fight and fight again to bring back sanity and honesty and dignity, so that our Party with its great past may retain its glory and greatness.

He was given a standing ovation—in which at least four members of the platform and about a third of the delegates

did not join. Then, in a deadly hush, the chairman, Dick
Crossman, announced the results of the vote:

> For the Transport Union resolution   3,282,000
> Against   3,239,000

Cousins and the unilateralists had won by a hairs-breadth
majority—43,000. Pandemonium broke out as the left-wing
delegates cheered and cheered and cheered again. Gaitskell,
looking white and weary, slipped off the platform.

The next night the Transport Union held its traditional
conference dinner, at which Gaitskell, as Leader, was guest
of honour. George Brown did his best to introduce a party
spirit, but the Gaitskells and the Cousinses barely spoke to one
another. Hugh Gaitskell, the eternal Wykehamist, attempted
the usual courtesies, but Nance Cousins, according to eye-
witness observers, displayed open hostility.

Cousins did not get the opportunity at the party conference
(where, unlike the TUC, the mover does not have the right of
reply) to answer Gaitskell's questions and explain where he
stood on NATO and the Western alliance. Had he done so,
it is doubtful whether he would have thrown any light on the
matter. His views have usually been shrouded in ambiguity.
Canon Collins, during those long marches from Turnham
Green to Trafalgar Square, discussed politics at length with
him, but very much later the Canon could not recall whether
Cousins had gone as far as the CND leadership in wanting to
pull out of NATO. 'I don't think he ever said so,' he told me.
'It was the Bomb he was against—that was the dominating
factor—to get rid of the Bomb.'

The Bomb indeed had become almost an obsession. As
Trevor Evans noted in the *Daily Express*:

> Frank Cousins has reached a point where his convictions
> about the abolition of the H-bomb are so deep that no-
> thing else matters.

To him it was an emotional and moral rather than a political or strategic issue. He could be described as a unilateralist but not a neutralist. He was never a pacifist, and had no use for the extremist brash 'Yankees go home' factions. In his own speech at Scarborough he had dodged the issue:

> When I am asked if it means getting out of NATO, if the question is posed to me as simply saying, am I prepared to go on remaining in an organisation over which I have no control, but which can destroy us instantly, my answer is Yes, if the choice is that, but it is not that.

Soon after the conference he was pressed on TV for his views. He replied:

> There is no reason at the moment why we should get out of NATO. But I would rather have NATO as it was intended to be, a defensive instrument against aggression, without threatening the use of nuclear weapons.

Hugh Gaitskell went ahead with his threat to fight and fight and fight again. Harold Wilson, who had sat sphinx-like on the platform puffing away at his pipe throughout the defence debate, decided to run for the party leadership. He is said to have consulted a colleague: would it be a good thing for him to throw in his lot publicly with the CND? But the issue on which he fought was Gaitskell's doctrine that party conference decisions were not binding on the Parliamentary party. (Six years later he came round to Gaitskell's point of view.) Wilson secured 81 votes to Gaitskell's 166 in the Parliamentary party ballot that autumn, and this probably represented the sum total of the left's strength in the House of Commons.

Secure in the Parliamentary party, Gaitskell planned to consolidate his position in the wider movement. The Campaign for Democratic Socialism (originally christened Victory for Sanity) was formed on October 19th, with Bill Rodgers, former secretary of the Fabian Society, as its organiser. The CDS adopted the infiltration tactics of the other side, bombarding union branches and local constituency parties with ammunition in the shape of leaflets, bulletins and information material. The split in the CND itself played straight into its hands.

Meantime, the party executive set about drawing up yet another statement on defence policy to put before the 1961 conference. This time Crossman and Walter Padley, the shop workers' President, were the architects. The statement did not please Gaitskell at all, though it succeeded in winning back many of the unions which had gone unilateralist.

But not Frank Cousins. He and his union stuck faithfully to their unilateralist line, though at their 1961 conference at Brighton the minority was more vocal than in previous years. George Brown, who was rooting for the official policy, asked that, as a union official, he might be allowed to address the delegates on behalf of the TGWU Parliamentary group. Cousins icily refused, invoking the union rule book: 'As an officer of the Union, Brother Brown knows as well as I do that it would be unconstitutional.'

Brown held a meeting of his own in the Dome, on the Sunday evening, and declared: 'It is the duty of those of us who hold different views from the General Secretary to express them.' The meeting was poorly attended and was picketed by militant busmen who distributed leaflets telling Brother Brown, in unfraternal and un-Parliamentary language: 'If Mr Brown will mind his own bloody business we promise to mind our own bloody business.'

When it came to the TUC and the party conference in the autumn the trade union block votes swung Gaitskell's way. The TGWU resolution was defeated by 2,418,00 votes at the Blackpool party conference. This marked the beginning of the decline of the Campaign for Nuclear Disarmament as a force within the Labour party, and the ascendancy of Hugh Gaitskell as party leader.

11

'Old-fashioned Socialist'

A COLLEAGUE who has known the Cousins family well from early days told me: 'The trouble about Frank and Nance is that they are still living in the atmosphere of the Doncaster Women's Co-op Guild of the 1930s.' Cousins would not necessarily take this as a stricture. He has described himself as an 'old-fashioned Socialist', and has always been inordinately proud of his working-class background and of the fact that his roots lie deep in the Labour movement. He has consistently attacked the honours system and on a BBC 'Any Questions' programme in January 1959 said:

I don't believe in the thing, and I am not likely to be tempted to change my beliefs. I think it is wrong that people from our side who are opposed to the system of privilege join in the acceptance of privileges.

Once he was asked whether he would become a knight. He exploded:

Don't think that I'll ever accept a knighthood. I don't care what the others do. Not me. Not Frank Cousins, never.

Robert Willis recalls a curious conversation in the late 1950s while they were pacing up and down the corridor in the Treasury waiting for a Tory Chancellor to receive a TUC deputation. 'Have you any political ambitions, Bob?' asked Cousins.

Willis replied, 'My only ambition is not to join the ranks of the TUC knights.'

'Well, that makes two of us,' was Cousins' rejoinder.

His own definition of Socialism, given in a TV 'Face to Face' interview with John Freeman in 1961, was:

> The protection of the right of the ordinary people to have opportunity, security and education for the standard they are fitted to take, and all the opportunities we want for our own children. I don't want Capitalism to have control of the right to work, or the right to live, or the right to have a place to go to. I want a new order of things.

Cousins' Socialism is emotional and instinctive, and comes from his heart as much as his brain. He mistrusts those who do not share his views and is suspicious of intellectuals, whether of the right or the left. He did not take sides in the Bevanite controversies which rent the Labour movement in the 1950s.

He had for a brief period, as TGWU Assistant General Secretary, filled one of the twelve trade union seats on the Labour National Executive. Even at that early stage he used to express impatience at the tendency of the politicians to indulge in theoretical arguments and personal feuds. Cousins was on the NEC at the time of the Margate conference in 1955 when Harold Wilson's report on party organisation was discussed in private session. Wilson had likened the Transport House machine to a 'penny farthing in a jet age' and the debate attracted a great deal of attention.

To hold a secret session on any controversial issue is a sure way of ensuring maximum publicity and Margate 1955 was no exception. The fact that the windows overlooking the promenade were left open so that the loudspeakers carried every word to holiday-makers made it as public a gathering as if it had been held on the beach.

Bevan was the centre of interest and he let fly at the Wilson report. What was wrong with the party, he said, was not its machinery but its policy, which was barely distinguishable from that of the Tories. Cousins much later was to make the same criticisms, but at this conference his intervention in the debate was concerned with such mundane matters as the need for proper canvassing and marked registers. His speech went unnoticed in the next day's papers.

Cousins was never particularly close to Aneurin Bevan. I remember one evening during the Labour party conference at Blackpool in October 1956 we were having a drink in the Imperial Hotel with Bevan. He was in a rather sullen mood and was evidently still smarting from his recent defeat by Gaitskell for the party leadership. He was also on tenterhooks, awaiting the outcome of the election for party treasurership, in which he was standing against George Brown. Cousins and his wife walked into the lounge and came over to our table. There was a sudden lowering of voices and everybody in the room looked round expectantly. Bevan was still very much the leader of the political left and Cousins had, only a few weeks before, emerged as the hero of the trade union militants. Would this, their first meeting since Cousins' TUC speech, produce the seeds of an alliance between the two leading left-wing 'rebels'? In the event, the encounter was brief and rather bleak. The two men exchanged polite greetings, but there was no sign that they were on the same wave-length.

Bevan defeated Brown by 3,029,000 votes to 2,755,000. From that moment he began to move away from his former left-wing allies and come to terms with Gaitskell, who that autumn gave him the job he coveted of Shadow Foreign Secretary.

Bevan, who had always bitterly attacked the trade union block vote, found that when it went his way it was not without its redeeming features. Cousins always defended the block vote as being democratic. He once pointed out that his union's one million vote was only cast at the party conference, after full discussion, whereas a constituency party's 1,000 card could be held up at the whim of the individual delegate. This is not necessarily so. In my own experience as a delegate to the conference, the local General Management Committee mandates the representative on most major issues and since GMC members are likely to be more politically articulate than the average members of a TGWU branch, the way the delegate votes undoubtedly reflects the wishes of the local party membership.

A fairer criticism which Cousins might have made, and one which Herbert Morrison was very fond of making, is that as 1,000 members is the minimum affiliation for an individual party, a constituency with only 250 paid-up members votes on behalf of 750 non-existent voters. The late Ian Mackay pointed out: 'The TWGU vote may represent sheep, but they are real sheep, not the kind of sheep you count in your sleep.'

On many issues Cousins' line has been supported by the Communists, and, some might say, has been indistinguishable from theirs. But Cousins has never had any use for the British Communist party and has always rejected the view that the end justifies the means. A man of his individualistic and independent temperament could never submit to the mental disciplines which bind Communists in steel hoops to the prevailing line. He is a staunch Social Democrat, who looks to the Scandinavian, rather than to the Soviet system, as the model for British Socialists.

Many people were surprised when, early on in his leadership, he upheld the rule which Deakin imposed in 1948, banning Communists (and Fascists) from holding official positions in the Union. Though privately he thought at the time the rule was 'daft' and only drove the militants into open opposition, he advised his union's rules revision conference not to alter it. There were frequent suggestions that the TUC should re-establish formal links with the Communist-led World Federation of Trade Unions. Cousins always resisted these pressures.

He had planned a visit to Russia in 1956, much to the

alarm and despondency of the TUC General Council, but cancelled it because of the events in Hungary. Since that date there have been many TGWU delegations to 'Iron Curtain' countries. It is significant that in the spring of 1967, when he was paying a visit to the USA, Cousins suggested that it would be a good idea to arrange for an invitation from one of the American transport unions, and thus show the world that the Transport Union did not take sides in the Cold War.

Hugh Gaitskell had become Leader of the Labour party in December 1955. At the start his relations with Cousins were cordial, and Cousins told the *Daily Herald* in 1956:

> Hugh Gaitskell has demonstrated to everyone not only that he is able to lead, but that he has the Labour movement, the party and the unions behind him.

The two men were drawn close together politically over the Suez crisis, even though they had no personal associations. (I remember Cousins ringing me at home one night to ask for Gaitskell's home phone number, so that he could discuss the Suez situation urgently.)

The Brighton Labour party conference in 1957 was the scene of a dramatic reconciliation between Gaitskell and Bevan. In the opening days of the conference Cousins seemed to be playing ball. I wrote in the *News Chronicle*: 'A Gaitskell-Bevan-Cousins axis is being forged', and that this would ensure party unity at the next general election. This judgment was very wide of the mark. A deep split developed over the Bomb, and the feuding broke out all over again.

Frank Cousins originally voted in favour of Gaitskell's policy document, 'Industry and Society', which set out a plan for State investment in private industry. He did so, he explained, on the understanding that this was complementary to, and not a substitute for, outright public ownership. Early in the autumn of 1958, when he attacked the official party policy on public schools as 'going back on our Socialism', he was still ready to come to terms. He expressed gratitude to Gaitskell for his support during the London bus strike.

'Thank you, Frank,' said Gaitskell. Cousins replied: 'We shall be critical, but we are with you. We expect socialist thinking from the political side, in return for co-operation from the trade unions.'

Cousins must have become convinced that the Leader's thinking was not sufficiently Socialist because at his own union conference the following summer we find him launching a frontal attack on Gaitskell's home and foreign policies. This conference, which met at Douglas, Isle of Man, in July 1959, rejected the 'Industry and Society' plan by a huge majority, after Cousins had said it was not 'true Socialism'. He was delighted to receive a telegram from Labour MPs Emanuel Shinwell and George Wigg:

> Congratulations on your reaffirmation of the principles of public ownership and your repudiation of the idea of buying shares in private companies. You are a good Socialist.

This was followed by a second telegram, from Herbert Morrison, Ellis Smith and Arthur Lewis: 'Gladly add our names.' Cousins told his delegates:

> Their telegrams are welcome. . . . There has been a little too much tendency on the part of some people to go around trying to explain away the beliefs we hold in public ownership, as if to make it clear to the employing groups that we don't intend it.

One delegate, Tom Fitzpatrick, a London busman, warned that Cousins was endangering the prospect of a Labour Government being returned. Cousins retorted that the movement thrived on debate, and it was utterly wrong to talk about a split. Fitzpatrick's views were clearly shared by many in the Labour party. When the general election of 1959 produced a disastrous defeat for Gaitskell, Cousins was openly blamed for causing the split. He himself had campaigned vigorously for all the TGWU candidates, whether of the right or the left, and had spoken for George Brown. But the damage to the party 'image' as a coherent and cohesive force had already been done.

The 1959 defeat and its aftermath produced a wave of real bitterness within the Labour party, and the delegates met to lick their wounds at Blackpool during a wet November weekend. It was here that Gaitskell flew his kite about dropping Clause Four, the 'public ownership' clause in the party constitution:

> It seems that this needs to be brought up to date. . . . It lays us open to continual misrepresentation. It implies that the only precise object we have is Nationalisation whereas we have many other Socialist objectives. It implies that we propose to nationalise everything, but do we? . . . Let us remember that we are a Party of the future, not of the past.

Gaitskell was thinking aloud, courageously, if ill-advisedly, and was saying things which the majority of party members privately agreed with. But he saw his kite shot down in flames by trade unionists and left-wing delegates alike. Cousins came out flatly against any soft-pedalling of public ownership. 'It would be wrong to trim our sails to any prevailing electoral wind, and unsuccessful too,' he wrote in his union journal. He kept up a relentless campaign. In March 1960 he told the Bristol Regional Festival:

> We are not going to run away from our principles in order to get votes.

A few months later, at Perth, he said:

> If some of the élite of the party can define it [Clause Four] as saying that it will be kept in to satisfy the fuddy-duddies and sentimentalists of the unions, we in our union will be proud to join the ranks of the sentimentalists and

fuddy-duddies because we are proud of our belief in Clause Four. . . . We have never thought that the most important job the politicians do is to return themselves to the House of Commons.

He was, however, irritated by the tendency to personalise the conflict as one between Gaitskell and himself. It was not the Cousins line, but that of the Union, he insisted, saying:

I have no personal antagonism towards the Leader of the Labour party and I am sure he has none towards me. What I think is that he is mistaken in his philosophies. They are not, in my opinion, Socialist beliefs.

Faced with mounting opposition, Gaitskell dropped his plan to re-write Clause Four, and give the Labour party a 'modern mid-twentieth-century image'.

By one of the ironies of history it was left to Harold Wilson, who had never been an ally of Gaitskell and indeed opposed him for the leadership in 1960, quietly to 'bury' Clause Four. The Wilson Government clearly established the doctrine, without spelling it out, that the Labour party accepted a 'mixed' economy.

Hugh Gaitskell realised that he had been isolated and decided to retreat over Clause Four in order to concentrate on winning the, to him, much more important battle over defence. The fundamental conflict between him and Cousins was not over any semantic definition of Socialism, but over the issue of nuclear disarmament which came to overshadow all others between 1959 and 1961.

The story of the bitter clash over the Bomb and defence policy was told in the last chapter. But before leaving the subject of Cousins' relations with the Leader of the party we may be permitted to jump ahead to a remarkable supper party on November 12th, 1962, a few months before Gaitskell's death. By then the issue of the Bomb was more or less out of the way and the scars were beginning to heal. Gaitskell apparently decided that it was time for a *rapprochement* with Cousins, and invited him and Nance to his Hampstead home to talk things over. The supper party *à quatre* was a great success and after the meal Gaitskell mentioned that he was thinking about his next Cabinet, and indicated that a place would be found for Cousins. It was all very tentative and no precise job was mentioned, but Gaitskell was known to have the Ministry of Transport in mind. Cousins was undoubtedly pleased at the suggestion, though neither he nor his wife took it particularly seriously. Just before Christmas he went out of his way to praise Gaitskell's leadership at a union gathering. Some of his officials who had not yet caught up with the situation were astonished to hear him. The acute political correspondent of *The Times*, David Wood, however, had gathered that something was in the wind. He noted in his contribution to a memorial symposium on Gaitskell:

> By some accounts, Gaitskell just before his death had begun to heal the breach with Cousins and the two men might have eventually found a *modus vivendi* that would have prevented further dangerously destructive clashes.

It is to Gaitskell's credit that he eventually sought to come to terms with Cousins. It is to his discredit that he waited so long and allowed so much bad feeling to be engendered before doing so. It will always remain something of a puzzle why the party Leader did not at an earlier stage seek to moderate the growing hostility of the most powerful man in the trade union movement. It was no good repining and wishing for the good old days of Arthur Deakin—Cousins was there, larger than life, a force to be reckoned with.

Gaitskell and Cousins were temperamentally and personally out of sympathy. Both shared the same quality of sincerity and the same defect of obstinacy. A mutual incompatibility had developed not only between them but between their wives. The Cousinses were suspicious of the idea that the

'Hampstead Set' was shaping party policy at Sunday morning sessions or over the dinner table, and resented the effortless intellectual superiority which seems so frequently to be the hallmark of Wykehamists.

In politics nothing is immutable, but I do not personally think that the reconciliation could have lasted. If Harold Wilson, with his superior political sense and capacity to handle awkward colleagues, failed to keep Cousins in the fold, it is highly unlikely that Gaitskell would have succeeded. Not only was Gaitskell lacking in subtlety but he would certainly have been far more dogmatic about the need to uphold the prices and incomes policy.

Wilson's election as party Leader after Gaitskell's death in January 1963 brought about a further change of alignment. Wilson had never been particularly close to Cousins or the Transport Union, but he recognised that the party had to be led from somewhere 'left of centre', and that this involved good working relationships with one of the most powerful influences on the left. The two seemed to share parallel views on industrial and technological matters, and Cousins campaigned vigorously for Wilson during the 1964 election, sharing his eve-of-poll platform. An effective partnership was forged—though it was not at first clear who was going for the ride, and who was the tiger!

I

12

The corridors of power

Harold Wilson's decision to bring Cousins into his Cabinet as Minister of Technology was the biggest surprise of the long Ministerial list he announced on the morrow of the 1964 election. Wilson had taken careful steps to safeguard his left flank by including those who had been his associates in the Bevanite group, for example Richard Crossman and Barbara Castle, and had been liberal in dispensing undersecretaryships to potential rebels. Many saw the appointment of Cousins as the Prime Minister's master-stroke in the process of consolidating his position, a subtle, if not Macchiavellian, move to 'nobble' a man who, as Britain's most powerful trade union leader, might have been dangerous outside. In fairness, Cousins had shown that he was a consistent advocate of industrial modernisation, as well as a good administrator, so his appointment to this particular Ministry was not altogether without logic.

The surprise lay not so much in the offer as in his acceptance of it. Cousins had persistently and publicly denied any desire to enter Parliament and only a few months before the election said:

> I have told the man who will be picking the next Cabinet that I have an important job to do where I am. I am staying in the trade union movement.

One rumour was that the bargain was struck over a picnic lunch in the Scilly Isles in August 1964, when Frank and Nance Cousins were spending their holiday in Cornwall and went over to visit the Wilsons. But there is reason to believe that the agreement was reached later during the campaign.

Both Harry Nicholas, his number two, and Bill Jones, the Union's busman vice-president, advised Cousins against going into the Government. They knew he was not a good politician, and thought—rightly as it turned out—that he would not be happy in the House of Commons. They told him he could do a better job for the Labour movement if he stayed outside. This advice was singularly disinterested on Nicholas's part, for he, of all people, would stand to gain most from Cousins' departure from the Union. But Cousins had already made up his mind.

The union executive on October 17th gave him leave of absence without pay, on the understanding that he could return at any time. This provision is important in the light of later events. The Union issued a statement, supporting his request: 'He would feel the temporary parting most keenly, having regard to his long and active association at all levels. On the other hand, the problems were so big and the needs of the country too urgent for anyone to stand back—and it was in that spirit that he requested and we granted leave of absence.' Cousins himself told his executive members:

> The only thing that made me do it was the suggestion that I was needed to play a part in the drive to resolve our economic problems and get production going by using scientific methods and technological advance.

He described his new role as 'a stirring new venture . . . fascinating and exciting'. His union colleagues, he said, agreed with him that the new job was 'an extension of my work for the movement'.

> Many have told me that if I did as good a job for the country as I have done for the Union, then my move will be amply justified. This is a challenge to me personally. It is also a responsibility for the whole of the movement. We have the opportunity to prove that our criticisms of in-

efficient Government were right, and we must now try to give the country the leadership it needs.

After the meeting, some of the members of the union executive adjourned to the Marquis of Granby opposite Transport House for a drink and a sandwich. There they ran into Barbara Castle and her husband Ted and told them the decision. 'Thanks, lads, for letting us have him,' said Barbara Castle.

It was in a mood of supreme confidence and dedication that Cousins, who had just celebrated his sixtieth birthday and had only recently recovered from a severe heart attack, embarked upon a completely new career. The disillusionment which eventually followed was made all the greater by his early hopes of success.

The Ministry of Technology was born on October 17th, 1964, in a room in the Paymaster-General's office in Whitehall. Five men acted as midwives: Cousins; Sir C. P. (later Lord) Snow, his Parliamentary Secretary; Sir Maurice Dean, Permanent Secretary; Professor Patrick Blackett, FRS; and Christopher Herzig, the Minister's private secretary. They had to build up a department from literally nothing and scratch round not only for staff and premises but for furniture and fittings. Staff was a particularly acute problem, because the other new Ministry, the Department of Economic Affairs, had got in first with recruiting economists and Civil Servants and was creaming off the best men for itself. George Brown knew the Whitehall ropes, while Cousins was a complete outsider. Indeed one of his Ministerial colleagues told me it was a 'crying shame' to give him a non-existent department where he did not have a galaxy of talented and experienced Civil Servants to guide him.

After about a week, the Ministry, with a skeleton staff, installed itself in the eighth floor of Millbank Tower, the skyscraper headquarters of the Vickers Group. Cousins himself has recalled:

To begin with I was the Ministry. I had to go and look for a secretary to get a letter typed, and if I wanted a cup of tea, I had to get a porter to make me one.

He even had to wait five months before he received his Ministerial salary—this was because there was no financial provision for all the new departments created—and it was several months before he could answer personally for his department in the House of Commons. Until his election at Nuneaton on January 21st, 1965, Parliamentary questions were answered for him by H. G. Boyden, one of the Parliamentary under-secretaries to the Department of Education and Science.

Recruiting the right staff was not the only difficulty in those early days. An even more fundamental problem arose from the lack of guidance about the Ministry's precise functions. It was grandiloquently envisaged as a spearhead of the drive to create a new Britain—'the Britain that is going to be forged in the white heat of the scientific revolution', as Harold Wilson told the Labour party conference in 1963. The Ministry, Wilson promised, would 'mobilise scientific research in this country in producing a new technological breakthrough' and 'make us once again one of the foremost industrial nations of the world'.

The Prime Minister on November 20th outlined the Ministry's very broad terms of reference as 'general responsibility for guiding and stimulating a major national effort to bring advanced technology and new processes into British industry'. But just how it was to set about this task, how it would be organised in practice and what would be its range of responsibilities were never clearly spelled out.

The old Ministry of Education which had become a department and had the magic words 'and of Science' added to it in April 1964, had already embarked on its own empire-building. Where did science end and technology begin? What were the precise dividing lines between the two departments?

These sort of questions led to interminable arguments. Cousins was not used to this kind of Whitehall in-fighting, and was accustomed to being at the head of a well-established organisation. At Transport House decisions had to be taken on concrete day-to-day problems, but at the Ministry, before it had established itself, the issues were nebulous and ill-defined. Cousins would undoubtedly have been far happier if Gaitskell's idea of making him Minister of Transport had materialised and he could have dealt with practical matters like building roads and bridges and running trains. 'You'll be all right when there's a flow of work coming on to your desk and there's some concrete stuff you can get your teeth into', one of his Civil Servants said comfortingly.

For all the initial difficulties, Frank Cousins threw himself into the job of building up a Government department with great energy and enthusiasm. One of his first acts was to appoint a high-powered Advisory Council on Technology, with Professor Blackett as his deputy chairman. The Council's terms of reference were: 'To advise on the application of advanced technology in British industry'. The Minister succeeded in enlisting the services of eight men, drawn from the very top ranks of the industrial and academic worlds. These included Sir Leon Bagrit (Elliott Automation), Sir William (now Lord) Carron (AEU President), Mr C. F. (now Sir Frank) Kearton (Courtaulds), Lord Nelson of Stafford (English Electric), Mr H. C. (now Sir Hugh) Tett (Esso Petroleum), Sir Arnold Hall (Hawker-Siddeley) and the Vice-Chancellors of Lancaster and Strathclyde Universities. Cousins was delighted that everybody he approached agreed to serve. When he first drew up his list, officials demurred: 'They're all too busy.' Cousins replied: 'I want busy men.' He got on extremely well with these outside advisers, especially the industrial tycoons whom he had so often met on the other side of the negotiating table. They talked the same language and had the same pragmatic approach to technical problems.

The growth of the Ministry of Technology is almost a text-book example of Parkinson's Law. From a 'man and a boy' basis it steadily built up an empire. It took over ministerial responsibility for the Atomic Energy Authority in January 1965, and enlarged its field to cover non-atomic work, including a major programme for desalination research and development. The National Research Development Corporation (the body which had pioneered the Hovercraft) followed in February, and its resources were raised from £10 to £25 million. But it was not until April 1965, six months after its creation, when it absorbed the industrial responsibilities of the Department of Scientific and Industrial Research, that the Ministry could be said to have found its feet and claim proper Whitehall status. It acquired a staff of 'boffins', who worked in the ten DSIR research stations and laboratories on a variety of problems, ranging from building to fish preservation. The doyen of these institutions was the National Physical Laboratory, which had been opened by George V, then Prince of Wales, in 1900. George V prophetically declared:

> I believe that we have the first instance of the State taking part in scientific research. . . . Does this not show that the nation is beginning to recognise that if its commercial supremacy is to be maintained, greater facilities must be given for furthering the application of science to commerce and industry?

It was to take sixty-six years to complete the process of State participation in science.

From the start, the Ministry had been made 'sponsor' department for four key industries with particular relevance to modern technology: machine-tools, computers, electronics and telecommunications. In December 1965 the mechanical and electrical engineering industries were added to the list. By the time Cousins left the Ministry in July 1966 it had an annual budget of £24½ million and a total staff of 5,600, of whom the vast majority were scientists and technologists, working in laboratories and research stations all over the country. The London staff numbered about 700, with only 200 at Millbank. In June 1966 it was announced that the Ministry's empire would be further enlarged, to take in the shipbuilding and aviation industries. This move was finally accomplished in February 1967, after Cousins had left. Almost overnight the Ministry's staff was swollen to 23,000.

Some people think it might have been difficult for Cousins with his known views on defence policy to become responsible for aviation, which impinges so closely on defence matters and where the borderline between civil and military research is blurred. This could, of course, apply equally to atomic energy and to many other sectors which came within his province. He himself always stressed the objective of harnessing scientific and technological resources to peaceful purposes.

The announcement of his new and enlarged responsibilities led Harold Hutchinson to comment in the *Sun*:

> Mr Cousins has become in everything but name the chief Minister of Industry—the most powerful figure in industry.

A rather less friendly note was struck by Chapman Pincher in the *Daily Express*:

> The lumbering elephant called the Ministry of Aviation is to be replaced by a floundering whale called the Ministry of Technology.

The Ministry of Technology was undoubtedly 'oversold' at the beginning, and the public expected spectacular, almost science-fiction results. The fact that it had such a controversial figure at its head brought it under perpetual scrutiny. Cousins was dogged by the press in much the same way that Aneurin Bevan had been pursued by reporters, when he was

Minister of Health in the 1945–50 Government. One typical example was the furore in one or two newspapers about Cousins' alleged luxurious private bathroom in Millbank Tower. This turned out to be completely mythical, but the tale earned him the title of 'prisoner in the bathroom'.

The Ministry was severely, and many thought unfairly, criticised by the Select Committee on Estimates in July 1965, which accused it of being 'top-heavy, slow, fear-provoking and staffed with the wrong people'. *The Times*, commenting on this report, said: 'After nine months Mr Cousins has little to show and his Ministry is regarded as a weak link in the Government's chain.'

It will be a long time before any worthwhile assessment of the effectiveness of the Ministry of Technology under Frank Cousins' leadership can be made, because of the long-term and experimental nature of most of its activities. Cousins himself was irritated by people who clamoured for quick results. He said in May 1966:

> We are laying the foundation for something that will change the face of British industry. It is a slow process because it is a vast problem. But in ten years' time nobody will ever remember when people asked, 'What is the Ministry of Technology doing?' What they are doing will be visible wherever you look.

The Ministry's first-aid treatment probably saved the British computer industry from collapse, while the establishment of a computer advisory service and the national computing centre at Manchester provided valuable practical help to management. The department encouraged the installation of advanced machine tools and developed the international alignment of standards (particularly important in view of Britain's later application to join the Common Market). It set up a service for the calibration of measuring equipment and developed a mobile production engineering service to show smaller firms how to improve their processes and develop low-cost automation. It made grants to forty-eight industrial research associations.

All this may not add up to the 'dynamic, purposive thrust' into the 21st century which Harold Wilson envisaged, but there is little doubt that in the first two years the seeds were sown for future development which Anthony Wedgwood Benn, a much less controversial figure with a greater flair for public relations, was able to exploit. Sir Maurice Dean, the Ministry's first Permanent Secretary, said in a lecture to the Royal Institute of Public Administration in November 1965:

> The Ministry of Technology has brought a new emphasis and a new orientation. It has brought into existence a point in Government under a Minister of Cabinet rank where the technological problems of industry are discussed in a scientific way.

Sir Maurice, who had served in the Foreign Office under Bevin, found himself at ease with the leader of a big trade union and was impressed at the rapidity with which Cousins settled into the job. He told me: 'I think that the idea of harnessing such a man to the task of modernising industry was really a stroke of genius.'

A very different assessment was made by Leslie Stone, in an article in *Socialist Commentary*, a middle-of-the-road Labour journal, in the summer of 1966:

> There is a feeling that more might have been accomplished. Not even the Ministry's best friends would claim that it has been a roaring success . . . The man in charge needs energy, drive, imagination, administrative skill and an evangelical, missionary fervour. The last Minister of Technology was deficient in most, if not all, of these qualities. It must be hoped that Anthony Wedgwood Benn can come closer to filling the bill.

The Ministry might have made a better impression if its Minister had been more alive to the importance of public relations or had been a better performer in Parliament. He made no secret of his dislike of the House and its procedural niceties, and tended to address the Chamber as if he were addressing a conference of his union. Throughout his Ministerial career he was mercilessly baited by Conservative backbenchers, who never let him forget his CND associations or his left-wing views on nationalisation. Good Parliamentary fun, perhaps, which a more experienced or less sensitive man would have shrugged off or returned in kind. But Cousins, used to captive audiences at a trade union conference, was badly rattled.

Bevin, it will be recalled, suffered the same experience when, at an equally advanced age, he became a Member of Parliament and a Minister. His officials at the Ministry reminded Cousins of Bevin's predicament and said, 'Ernie never liked the House, but he went through with it. So must you.'

It is tempting, and may be relevant, to recall the impact of Bevin's Parliamentary performances. According to Bullock:

He was awkward, either reading out an official brief in pedestrian fashion or when he spoke impromptu, often losing the thread of his argument and failing to catch the mood of the House. The formalities and procedure of Parliamentary debate irked him. Criticism which a practised parliamentarian accepted as the common form of debate, without allowing it to ruffle his temper, goaded Bevin to anger. He took it too personally and was too fierce in rebutting it. . . . These were faults which Bevin was slow to overcome: it was a long time before he felt at home in the House.

More than twenty years later another General Secretary of the Transport Union made his debut in the House of Commons with equally unfortunate results. Cousins' maiden speech, on February 19th, 1965, was described as a competent performance, though neither impressive nor imaginative. He kept his eyes glued to his brief, and one observer said of his delivery: 'It was as if a talking computer had run amok.'

His first appearance at Question time on March 2nd fills pages of *Hansard*. It was described by practised House of Commons hands as a 'near riot'. A clique of Tory back-benchers had tabled a long list of Questions, most of them loaded and intended to embarrass him rather than elucidate information about the rate of technological advance. They kept up a relentless barrage of supplementaries.

Would the Right Hon. Gentleman take steps to ensure the safety of the Aldermaston marchers? Does the Right Hon. Gentleman intend to make the journey to Aldermaston on foot? Would he visit the US Navy base at the Holy Loch? Did he share the views of a recent *Tribune* article on the nationalisation of the machine-tool industry? Why had he made such a political somersault in so short a time? And so on.

Twice the Minister had to be called to order for saying 'you' instead of 'the Hon. Member'. He apologised: 'No offence is intended, Mr Speaker. My experience in the past has been in directing thoughts to people who don't mind.' Quintin Hogg came gallantly to the rescue:

> Whilst I sympathise with the Right Hon. Gentleman as one who has recently made bad mistakes in addressing the House in the second person plural, and wish him the very best of luck in seeking to accustom himself, as I have had to do, may I ask him to realise that this (the progress of his Ministry) is a matter which is of very general interest in all quarters?

The Times Parliamentary correspondent described the scene:

> He looked . . . like a great chained bear. . . . Embarrassed and a trifle slow on his feet he aimed ungainly cuffs at the Tory terriers snapping round his heels. In they dashed and out again, baiting him cruelly with loaded questions about his CND activities and his views on nationalisation. . . .

In Parliamentary terms his maiden performance had been naive, inept and almost suicidal. Yet somehow he had emerged with his dignity intact. Perhaps the bear always does.

On the same day the Conservatives, supported in this instance by Sir Alec Douglas-Home, raised the constitutional propriety of a Minister of the Crown retaining his position as a trade union official. The Prime Minister himself defended Cousins and assured the House that there could be no possible conflict of interest since the Minister had cut himself off entirely from his trade union activities.

Despite his discomfiture in the House, Cousins was happy in the department itself, and worked extremely hard. He used to arrive at the office at about 8 a.m., to the consternation of his secretaries and officials, who were used to a more leisurely time-table. He would work late, and take papers home with him, unless he had to be in the House for a late division.

Cousins spent as much time as he could going round factories and visiting industries for which his Ministry was responsible. This he enjoyed. A member of his staff recalls: 'He was passionately interested in machines. He knew a good machine shop when he saw one, and a good apprentice scheme.' He would spend so long talking technicalities with the charge-hands and shop stewards that the organisers of his programme despaired of getting him through on time. Industrial managements, used to the somewhat superficial look round a workshop which most VIPs are content to bestow, must have experienced much the same kind of shock that Sir Frederick Burrows, former railwaymen's leader, administered to Indian diplomatic circles when he became Governor of Bengal in 1946: 'You're used to Governors who know all about hunting and shooting—now you've got a chap who knows all about shunting and hooting', he told them.

Cousins made several trips abroad, and visited both the USA and the USSR. He was a big success in America and got on well with the tycoons of the American computer industry and the top men at the Massachussetts Institute of Technology. The Russian trip in the summer of 1966 was extremely strenuous, involving a long air journey to see a scientific research centre in Siberia, factory visits from dawn till dusk and a number of highly technical discussions with Soviet Ministers, scientists and industrial managers. Cousins stood the strain very well, but used to become very fretful and irritable if anything went wrong in the programme, or upset the time-table. (The Russians' approach to a schedule is not always the same as that of Anglo-Saxons.)

He was popular with his Ministry staff, though some said 'he played his hand too close to his chest'. He tended to surround himself with a small group and rely exclusively on his two top officials, Sir Maurice Dean and Dr J. B. Adams, his scientific adviser. As in his TUC days, he was at his best in committee and in discussion with small groups. Members of his entourage recall: 'He was the life and soul of an office Christmas party.'

Cousins' chief contribution to the formative stage of the Ministry was perhaps his emphasis on human relations and the need for full consultation with the workers in introducing change. 'I can't be a dictator,' he said on his return from his Russian trip. 'I've got to persuade people to do things, just as I did when I was General Secretary of the Union.' He saw the problem of modernisation as 'persuading people to do things that they themselves knew ought to be done'. One of his most effective speeches was made to the conference of the Confederation of Shipbuilding and Engineering Unions at Torquay in June 1966. He appealed to trade unionists: 'Make it your business to get something done about productivity, so that greater efficiency and higher wages march in step, each one a spur to the other.' Union representatives, he said, should criticise and 'prod' managements into accepting new methods which would increase productivity.

13

The point of no return

ALL the time he was in the Cabinet Cousins studiously
avoided getting identified with the prices and incomes policy
which George Brown was, first jubilantly and later painfully,
hammering out. This policy soon became the cornerstone of
the Government's economic policy and Brown described it
in 1964 as 'the key to an economically growing and socially
just society'.

Brown who saw himself cast in the role of a latter day
Stafford Cripps, minus austerity, succeeded in getting employers and TUC leaders to join in signing the Declaration
of Intent on December 16th, 1964. This committed them to
co-operate with the Government in its prices and incomes
policy. His next step was to create the National Board for
Prices and Incomes, with the former Conservative MP,
Aubrey Jones, as Chairman and a mixed bag of members
drawn from industry and academic life, with a solitary trade
unionist, Robert Willis.

Even at this early stage, while the policy was still purely
voluntary, the Transport and General Workers' Union
registered opposition to it. A special TUC conference of
union executives on April 30th, 1965, endorsed the Declaration of Intent by the overwhelming majority of 6,649,000
votes to 1,811,000. Harry Nicholas, acting General Secretary
in Cousins' absence, cast the TGWU 1,400,000 votes with
the minority.

He did so, he explained, with 'reluctance'. In certain respects the policy was 'bold and imaginative' but the conditions

for its success were not present. 'Are we not seeking to introduce a policy without the means of achieving it?' he asked.
'As yet the economy remains unplanned.' He also warned
that it would constitute dangerous interference in the established system of wage bargaining.

How much the TGWU decision to oppose the policy was
influenced by the long shadow of Frank Cousins at Millbank
Tower must remain a matter of conjecture. Cousins certainly
did not breathe down the necks of the men who were holding
the fort just round the corner at Transport House, though,
undoubtedly, like Bevin, he kept himself informed. Even
when immersed in Foreign Office papers Bevin had kept a
watchful, if distant, eye on his successor and maintained his
private intelligence service.

Harry Nicholas once described Cousins' attitude as one of
'interest, not interference'. He has told me that he was never
in the least embarrassed at the thought that Cousins might
interfere, even though he kept a room in Transport House
where he conducted his constituency business. Cousins used
to attend regional rallies from time to time as an honoured
guest, but he was far too busy running a Government department to become involved in union routine.

In July 1965 the TGWU delegate conference at Portsmouth
carried a resolution rejecting the Government's prices and
incomes policy and opposing the whole concept of wage
restraint. Cousins paid a surprise visit to this conference.
Having sent a telegram to say he could not come, he turned
up unexpectedly, a sort of *deus ex machina*, on the closing
day. A move by a few branches to call for his resignation
from the general secretaryship, on the principle of 'one man,
one job', had been heavily defeated, and he received a tumul-
tuous ovation. He made a brief speech, replying to some of
his Tory critics:

> If anyone suggests that the way to prove I could be a
> good Cabinet Minister is to pretend that I did not and do

Above: 'The house didn't resign' (see page 148). The Cousinses' home at Carshalton Beeches. *Below:* Cousins at Blackpool with his wife Nance and daughter Frances

Left: Standing ovation for the Prime Minister at Blackpool TUC, 1966, in which Cousins and his colleagues did not join. *Below:* On the parade at Douglas, Isle of Man

not belong to the Transport and General Workers' Union, and that I am not part of the same struggle, then all I can say is that they will never understand us.

He went on to praise the delegates 'for having registered firm views about some matters of real concern'. As well as the resolution on wages, the conference had adopted a motion condemning the Government's policy on Vietnam. Cousins' congratulations to delegates for defying the Government on the twin pillars of its economic and foreign policies did not go unnoticed either by the press or by the Conservative opposition. On July 13th Mr Humphrey Atkins, MP for Merton and Morden, tabled a motion in the Commons regretting that the Minister of Technology 'appeared to encourage his union in its opposition to important aspects of Government policy for which, as a member of the Cabinet, he bears collective responsibility.' It was signed by forty Conservative MPs.

'Trojan Horse' . . . 'Silent enemy' . . . the epithets came thick and fast in the campaign to get Cousins to 'come clean'. The Leader of the Opposition, Edward Heath, said at Belfast on October 2nd:

A man can be loyal to his Cabinet colleagues. He can be loyal to his union comrades. But he cannot be loyal to both when they are on opposite sides of an industrial and political conflict. . . . I say to Mr Cousins, 'If you are a man of principle stand up and be counted. Resign from the Government or resign from the Union.' To Mr Wilson, I say 'If Mr Cousins is not prepared to choose his side, will you act? If you believe in the importance of the incomes policy, when are you going to get rid of Mr Cousins?'

At the Labour party conference that autumn Cousins sat with his union delegation in the body of the hall and remained seated when most of the conference delegates rose to their feet to cheer George Brown. This gave rise to a new

K

spate of speculation in the press and a new flood of invective from the Conservatives.

Cousins did not, however, lack defenders, and one of them, Lord Snow, his Parliamentary Secretary, said in the House of Lords that Cousins had been 'unfairly and absurdly attacked'. Richard Marsh, the able young trade union MP who later became Minister of Power and had been brought in to the Ministry of Technology in April 1965 to sustain Cousins in his Parliamentary ordeal, attacked the Tories for conducting an 'indecent campaign of innuendo against his personal integrity'.

Admittedly, Frank Cousins had placed himself in an equivocal position, given the doctrine of collective Cabinet responsibility. If he were to resign it would cut the Government's tenuous majority to only one—a number of deaths had reduced the figure from the original five—and it might look as if he had succumbed to the Tory attacks. He was at that time deeply absorbed in his Ministry, though it was an open secret that he would have liked to move to the Department of Economic Affairs and taken over responsibility for national planning. It was also well known that he was irked by the lack of co-operation from other departments in his plans for centralising Government purchases of British technical equipment. He had hoped to become a sort of overlord over Government spending on computers and automation equipment but found himself up against the brick wall of conservative Government departments.

At the beginning, bound together by the precarious Parliamentary majority and the euphoric sense that after thirteen long years in the wilderness the Socialist day was about to dawn, the members of Wilson's Cabinet were united in their determination to make a success of Government. 'We were an extraordinarily harmonious Cabinet, there was no ill-will and there were no bad personal relationships,' an ex-Minister ruminated. 'We were more harmonious than in Attlee's

Cabinet. Perhaps there weren't so many prima donnas.'

Cousins' relations with his fellow Ministers during the first Wilson Government were correct but never cordial. He was friendly with Anthony Greenwood, who was one of his union-sponsored MPs and a fellow left-winger. He had always been on good terms with Barbara Castle, but was said to be somewhat taken aback at her unabashed use of her feminine charm to get her way within the Cabinet. Richard Crossman, Minister of Housing, had been put in charge of scientific policy while the party was still in opposition, and it was expected that he would take over the Department of Education and Science. Instead, Michael Stewart was appointed. Cousins was disappointed and told Crossman that he had looked forward to working closely with him over the development of scientific and technological policies. He had very little in common with Stewart.

His relations with Ray Gunter, the Minister of Labour, were often very unhappy. 'That idiot Gunter,' he exploded, when, early on, he clashed with the Minister of Labour over his handling of a dispute in the London Docks. Gunter was a former President of the Transport Salaried Staffs Association, and Cousins resented the idea that a railwayman, and a white collar one at that, should intervene in a province which he still regarded as his own. Nor had he forgotten the incident at the Berne conference of the International Transport Federation, when the railway unions ousted him from the Presidency. Looking back, it is a pity that Cousins and Gunter could not have worked together. Both shared a passionate, almost puritanical, conviction about the ethical purpose of Socialism and both brought a practical trade union viewpoint into the Cabinet room. Cousins distrusted the 'intellectual' approach of many Ministers and complained that nobody thought about economic policy in terms of the people involved. 'They talk about it as if it was a Fabian lecture,' he said.

Nobody could accuse George Brown of being a 'Fabian intellectual', but he and Cousins had a long-standing feud. There has always been a 'love-hate' relationship between the two men, with what one observer described as 'brief excursions into friendship'. Brown was (and still is) an official of the union of which Cousins is General Secretary. They had grown up together, sparred, argued and fought each other for nearly thirty years. They had a common admiration for Bevin, though Cousins did not share Brown's high opinion of Deakin. Fundamentally they talked the same language, the language of trade union 'brothers', in contrast to the academic economists who thronged into Whitehall after the election.

At the time of their clash over defence policy Brown said: 'There is no bitterness on my part and no bitterness in the General Secretary. I regard Frank Cousins as a very great personal friend and I hope he regards me in the same way. But friendship cannot stand in the way of vigorous argument.' Politically, they remained poles apart and Brown to Cousins was the personification of the hated prices and incomes policy.

I have heard two conflicting versions of Cousins' attitude in the Cabinet, from two Ministers, one an intellectual, the other an ex-trade unionist. According to the intellectual Minister Cousins was always laying down the law and tended to treat the Cabinet much as if it were the TUC General Council, where he could indulge in arguing the finer points of policy with George Woodcock. According to this informant, Cousins did not master his Cabinet papers, but gave the impression of blundering through his briefs, and was always threatening to resign. At an early stage there was a suggestion that Dr (later Lord) Beeching might become an overlord of Transport. Cousins put his foot down, with the result that Beeching returned to ICI, whence he had originally come. 'The dismissal of Beeching was one of Frank's only real victories in the Cabinet,' this Minister commented.

The other (trade unionist) version is that Cousins was an impressive colleague in the Cabinet, who showed a grasp of his own technical subject. His characteristic attention to his 'homework', which had been revealed in his TUC days, stood him in good stead in the far more exacting atmosphere of the Cabinet room, and he more than held his own when any subjects involving technology were on the agenda. Yet he was strangely silent on many subjects on which, as a union leader, he had held such passionate views. According to this inform-ant Cousins felt himself at a disadvantage in discussing sub-jects on which he had not been briefed, and inadequately equipped to cross swords with, for example, the Chancellor, when it came to an argument about the pros and cons of devaluation.

'What did Cousins do or say about Vietnam?' I asked. This former Cabinet colleague said that, strangely, there was never any opportunity for a general debate on Vietnam policy, and explained that the procedure at a Cabinet meet-ing, unlike that of the TUC General Council, does not en-courage free-ranging discussion. 'We were always dealing with immediate issues and hearing reports about them. We never really had a good go at Vietnam. There was never any point in anybody trying to start up a debate, or making general attacks on policy,' he said.

Some people have said that Cousins did not fight hard enough within the Cabinet to promote the interests of his own department. This is hard to believe. He enjoyed the un-swerving support of the Prime Minister. 'If he had asked for the moon, Harold would have given it him,' a colleague commented. 'At one stage we were all roped in to help Cousins' department, and we all had to place orders for his computers.' There never seemed to be any difficulty from the Treasury about producing funds for technological ventures, and this may have irked Ministers who were constantly battling with the Chancellor for money for their own departments.

Cousins, after he resigned, said that the Cabinet was sometimes an 'irritant' to him, and that he was probably an 'irritant' to them. No doubt he was—and some of his colleagues would possibly have agreed with Sir John Elliot's remark: 'If he is lecturing the Cabinet to the same extent as he lectured me, he ought to claim overtime and Sunday rates.'

Cousins was a technical Minister and, as such, was circumscribed by his departmental duties. So too were Dick Crossman, at Housing, and Barbara Castle, first at Overseas Development and later at Transport. This preoccupation with their departments undoubtedly accounts for the failure of the former left-wingers to make an issue of foreign or defence policies which, in bygone days, they would have resisted, almost to the point of resignation. Even more, they were not anxious to be accused of 'rocking the boat'. Cousins deliberately eschewed politics in order to concentrate on the problems of technology.

The prices and incomes policy was an altogether different matter. This was something which was near to Cousins' heart, and involved a lifetime of experience and activity. As we have seen, he never gave any support to George Brown's efforts to establish a voluntary incomes policy, although his public identification with it would have been of inestimable value to the Government. He felt himself isolated—the practical trade union man in a crowd of economists and professional politicians who did not know at first hand the problems of the weekly pay packet or running a union branch. This was less than fair to lifelong trade unionists like Brown and Gunter, but Cousins, as so often on the TUC General Council, felt that he alone had his finger on the pulse of the trade union movement.

During the early discussions on the incomes policy his attitude was described by a senior colleague as one of 'smouldering and sullen hostility'. When it became clear that the Government meant to go ahead with compulsory measures, whatever Cousins said, hostility turned to vehement opposition. Time and time again he warned his Cabinet colleagues, 'The workers won't stand for it.' He warned them so often as to weary them into disbelief.

The Prices and Incomes Bill, in its first version, was published on February 24th, 1966, but lapsed with the dissolution of Parliament. The Bill was in three parts. Part 1 established the National Board for Prices and Incomes on a permanent and statutory footing. Part 2, to come into operation after the approval by Parliament of an Order in Council and after consultation with the TUC and the CBI, provided for the legal enforcement of the 'early warning' system in specified sectors of industry.

It placed the onus on a union, individual or employer to notify a claim, within seven days, and the onus on an employer to notify a settlement. There would be a standstill of thirty days before it could be implemented and if the Government referred it to the NBPI there would be a further standstill or 'cooling-off' period of up to three months. Penalties of fines would be imposed for infringement of any of the Bill's provisions.

The clause which angered Cousins most made it a punishable offence for a union to 'take or threaten to take any action by way of taking part or persuading others to take part in a strike, with a view to compel, induce or influence any employer to implement an award or settlement'. Part 3 dealt with non-controversial miscellaneous matters. The really controversial Part 4 was added later, after Cousins had resigned.

Cousins made no secret of his view that he could not remain a member of a Government which introduced penal sanctions against the unions. He was more than once on the verge of resignation, and was only held back by the knowledge that this might topple the Government. A colleague who was in his confidence warned the Prime Minister that if the Bill went through Cousins would walk out. 'I think you are probably right,' Wilson replied, and went out of his way to persuade Cousins to stay, at any rate till after the election, in order to preserve the party unity which was so essential to victory. Christopher Mayhew resigned without leaving a ripple, but Cousins was a very different proposition.

On March 11th, less than three weeks before polling day, there was this comment in *The Times*:

> Cousins is the senior Minister Mr Wilson can least afford to have resigning to become the standard-bearer for a coalition of left-wing critics, and the Minister who would have least to lose by resigning, because he is not a professional politician and could go back to union leadership.

Very much the same thought had occurred to Bevin when he was in the Government. He told his union conference in 1945:

> I have said to Arthur Deakin over and over again, 'Keep that chair there, just as it is!' As long as the fellows in 10 Downing Street know that I have that chair to fall into, my strength is added to. Do you think for one moment I could have held that office [Ministry of Labour] for five years if they hadn't known that, if they shot me out when I differed from them, there might be trouble outside?

At the general election of March 31st, 1966, the Labour party was returned with 363 seats against 253 for the Tories and 12 for the Liberals, an overall majority of 98. Cousins held Nuneaton with a greatly increased majority (11,403 compared with 5,241 at the 1963 by-election). He fought a vigorous campaign, but it was significant that his election address was confined entirely to his role as Minister of Technology and made no mention of the incomes policy or of the Prime Minister.

At an early stage in the campaign he seemed very despondent and, his agent recalls, almost on the point of giving up.

Then one of those mysterious happenings occurred which seem so characteristic of his career. One evening he received a long-distance call from Whitehall at his Nuneaton hotel. He came down to breakfast next morning, his old self, and told his friends, 'It's going to be all right.' The incident, vouched for by a source close to him during the election, serves to increase the mystery. What was 'it'? Was he given to understand that the Bill would be modified? Or that he would get the Department of Economic Affairs? Or was the whole thing a misunderstanding? The true story may never be known, as the only two people who could tell it are unlikely ever to do so.

The Prices and Incomes Bill was revived after the election, and the TUC economic committee was called in for consultation. Union leaders were left in no doubt that the Government, while accepting some of the amendments suggested by the TUC, was determined to push the Bill through as rapidly as possible.

The fact that Cousins was still in the Government, and back in his old job, led many people to assume that he had come to terms with Mr. Wilson. The *Daily Express* noted on April 13th: 'Frank Cousins is expected to agree to sever his link with the Transport and General Workers' Union' and reported a growing feeling that he would make way for his successor, whom everybody expected would be Harry Nicholas. The *Evening Standard*, the *Sun* and the *Daily Telegraph* reported in the same vein. When on June 9th Cousins paid a surprise visit to Transport House where the quarterly meeting of his executive was in session the rumours reached bursting-point. His immediate resignation was confidently expected. The usually well-informed and perspicacious industrial journalists turned out to be wrong in their predictions. Cousins did not resign from the Union.

Three days later a union official told a reporter: 'You would be correct if you said that Frank is prepared to leave the Cabinet and come back to us at any time that we feel his services are essential.'

On Saturday, June 17th, Cousins spoke at a Midlands Regional Festival at Trentham Park, near Stoke-on-Trent, when he made an important statement which was not picked up by the press. He said:

> I have no different views to those I had before I went into the Government and if steps are taken that are in too great a conflict with Union policy, there need be no doubt about where I shall stand and what I shall do.

A fortnight later he put this pledge into practice. At 11 a.m. on Sunday, July 3rd, he personally handed into Number 10 Downing Street a long letter of resignation. The following day, Monday, July 4th, the text of the Prices and Incomes Bill was published.

Since it is impossible to paraphrase this letter without losing its flavour and argumentation, and since it is so essential to an understanding of Cousins' activities before and after his resignation, the text is given in full:

Dear Harold,

Since joining the Government I have tried to persuade you and our Cabinet colleagues that the Prices and Incomes policy outlined in the Declaration of Intent and now accepted as the basis for a Parliamentary Bill is fundamentally wrong in its conception and approach.

The proposals in the Bill do not have any part to play in finding a solution of our economic problems, which are so obviously caused by our inability to create the additional productivity required in those sectors of industry which could help our balance of payments.

However well-meaning the original intentions of the architects of the scheme were, they have inevitably drifted into the state of believing that a policy of restricting wage increases is a substitute for an economic policy.

In our earlier talks on the subject, you agreed on the absolute necessity of developing a high wage level economy as the basis of prosperity, and you described the incomes restriction approach as the negative part of the planning, whilst the productivity and payments by results suggestions were the positive side.

In fact, just before the General Election you gave me to understand that you would help to break down the shibboleth of a belief that what we needed to secure economic recovery was sufficient power in the hands of the Government to compel the unions to accept without question the decisions of the Board for Prices and Incomes.

Unfortunately, you did not maintain that view and so our present policy has taken us into a position where disputes such as the recent strike of the seamen have been inevitable.

Other disputes will certainly occur and, because we are accepting the idea of a limited percentage norm of wage adjustment, the Government will be unable to follow its normal role of using the Ministry of Labour as a conciliation department, but will have reached a predetermined conclusion even before the dispute starts.

The NBPI [National Board for Prices and Incomes] is not, and cannot ever be, the correct body for determining the level of wages and conditions of employment over the whole range of salary and wage-earners in a democratic society, and any attempt to make the board such a body would create a pretence of adjudication whilst they would really be a rubber-stamping authority for previously determined Government decisions.

It is with regret that I see the present position being created, because I feel that both sides of industry were ready to co-operate with the Government in building a thriving, purposeful and wealthy society, but we have slipped back to the usual position of Treasury control of our approach to questions of investment spending and planning.

That attitude cannot help us in a drive towards expansion of demand and has obviously driven us to the position where our international monetary transactions have been based on assurances of our intention to restrict internal demand.

This is a wrong attitude and a contradiction of the

philosophy upon which our party is based and so it must be opposed.

Much of our domestic and external policy has been determined by the acceptance of that principle, which is so absolutely contrary to the views which I hold that I feel it would be better for both of us if you would accept my resignation from the Government.

When we first discussed my role in your team of Ministers I made it unmistakably clear that I could not support legislation that could have the effect of restricting the rights of the trades unions to present claims freely on behalf of their members, or to pursue such claims at any level to the best of their ability and take such steps legally and properly open to them to secure as quickly as possible the fair settlement of their claims.

This to my mind is one of the fundamental elements of a social democracy and I am sure that any restriction of those rights would lead us to a position where the Government would find it necessary to invoke legal sanctions against those who disagree with them.

I shall of course be very sorry to leave the Ministry of Technology, which has, through the efforts of some excellent and dedicated Civil Servants at all levels, aided by the help given by some splendid colleagues on the Advisory Council for Technology, the AEA [Atomic Energy Authority] and the NRDC [National Research Development Corporation] become a great instrument for assisting in the modernisation of British industry.

Many of the best firms in the important sectors of industry have already accepted the Ministry as partners in this task of building a better future, and it is my sincere hope that you will continue to regard the Ministry as a real means of improving the economic position of the country.

So, with a feeling of sorrow that the Government appears to be determined to push through a meaningless Prices and Incomes Bill, I ask you to understand why I feel I must leave you and return to my old job, where I shall at least have some chance of helping to create the atmosphere of voluntary co-operation between both sides of industry which is so necessary if we are to make progress

towards increased productivity and the planned growth of
wage levels we all said we wanted.

Sincerely yours,

Frank

The Prime Minister replied to Cousins:

Dear Frank,

Thank you for your letter which you brought to me this
morning. I do not need to repeat what I said to you in our
discussions how much I regret that you thought it necessary to come to this decision.

Certainly you have been completely consistent throughout on this matter and made plain to our colleagues and to
me your attitude to the Prices and Incomes Bill and the
action you felt you would have to take.

You know that I recognise the depth and sincerity of
your feeling on this matter. Only you can decide that it
represents the deep issue of principle requiring you to
resign from the Government, even though this is not, I
think, a view that your colleagues will share.

I do not propose to go into all the issues raised in your
very full and frank letter because we have discussed them
at some considerable length.

Neither our colleagues principally concerned nor I have
felt that prices and incomes policy can ever be a substitute
for a broader and more comprehensive economic policy
such as we are following.

As you know, in ministerial discussions and in a whole
succession of public speeches I have always described the
restraint required in the matter of prices and incomes as in
one sense a negative part of our general policy, increases in
productivity and the relation of pay to productivity being
the positive side.

But equally in those discussions and speeches I have
stressed that if we are not successful in relating prices and
incomes to national increases in productivity, we shall fail
in what is the cardinal element in our economic policy,
namely our determination to solve the nation's economic
difficulties while still maintaining full employment.

I cannot conclude this letter without thanking you, as I

have orally, for all you have done in creating the Ministry of Technology and in bringing it to the point where I believe we are now going to see real and growing results throughout British industry.

You can be assured that I shall continue to regard the Ministry as the essential element in improving the country's economic position and as the spearhead of our attack on the problem of modernising British industry.

Again, with regret for your decision but with good wishes for your future

Yours,
Harold

In spite of the friendly 'Dear Harold–Dear Frank' note, the correspondence between the two men strikes the outsider as somewhat cold-blooded. It is indeed difficult to depict the agonising choice which faced Frank Cousins during the three months between the election and July 3rd. He had all his life worked to see a Labour Government in power and yet, as he saw it, the Government was slipping off course and he was proving powerless to prevent it. For a highly emotional man like Cousins the final decision must have been a painful one.

Nearly a year later he casually mentioned in a BBC 'Any Questions' programme that excessive defence expenditure was one of the reasons why he had resigned. Those who have ploughed through his long letter will notice that there is not a single mention of defence in it. The argument was purely and simply about prices and incomes. In much the same way, Aneurin Bevan, when he resigned in 1951 over National Health Service charges, later widened the issue to embrace the whole of the Government's rearmament policy.

14

July 1966

THE news that Frank Cousins had resigned from the Government burst on a completely unprepared public. Only his closest associates or those who had read between the lines of his Trentham Park speech were not surprised. He rang up Harry Nicholas at home on Sunday morning, July 3rd, to tell him he had just been to Number Ten Downing Street to deliver the fateful letter. Most of his union officials heard the announcement for the first time on the BBC that evening. Bill Jones, the Vice-President, who only three weeks before had urged Cousins to return to the Union, exploded: 'Makes me look a proper Charlie!' It was the second time, he told me, that Cousins had 'made a monkey' of him. 'I'd told the press boys he wasn't going *in*, and then I told them he wouldn't be coming *out*.'

The Nuneaton Labour party was equally dumbfounded. Herbert Knight, its chairman, said: 'This has come as a complete surprise. I was with Frank Cousins a week ago and he never made any suggestions about resigning over the wages policy.'

The timing of his resignation is one of those mysteries which may never be completely cleared up. The *Guardian* noted:

> Only three weeks ago Cousins seemed determined to hang on to his Cabinet post. What, in those three weeks, could have changed his mind?

The Prices and Incomes Bill was actually published on Monday July 4th, the day after he resigned. It must, however, have been in draft, and possibly even in print, for some time before.

I have asked many people close to the scene: 'What happened between June 9th when Cousins didn't resign, and July 3rd, when he did?'

'Nothing' was the terse, and probably true, answer I received from one who was very much involved in events. Cousins' fellow Ministers knew that he was bound to go, and that it was only a matter of time before he took the plunge. It is conceivable that Cousins, having consulted his closest associate at Transport House, Jack Jones, deemed it advisable from an internal union point of view to delay the moment of his return. Had he announced his intention in June it might have looked as if he had succumbed to left-wing pressure, instead of choosing his own time. On the other hand, if he decided to stay in the Government it would be necessary to hold a fresh election for a new General Secretary. Nobody particularly wanted this, especially as an election was in any event due in 1969 when Cousins reached the retirement age of sixty-five.

Another suggestion was that he had grown very fond of his constituency and did not want to let the Nuneaton people down, or involve them in yet another Parliamentary election so soon after the general election.

Many other interpretations have been given, some less plausible, some less charitable. It was suggested to me that Cousins was concerned about his superannuation rights, but this seems to have been without foundation; and also that he was anxious to lead the Union once more before he retired, and did not want Harry Nicholas to step into his shoes. (It is tempting here to draw a parallel with Attlee's determination not to let Herbert Morrison succeed him, and Harold Macmillan's cavalier treatment of R. A. Butler. In all three cases the second-in-command was in the same age-group as the leader and had only narrowly missed getting the top job.

Both Morrison and Butler had held the fort while their Prime Ministers were abroad, or ill, and Harry Nicholas had actually occupied the General Secretary's seat for some twenty months. Nicholas, however, is far too unassuming a man, and too loyal, to harbour resentment or to complain about the slings and arrows of outrageous fortune.)

Some observers—and I must confess to having been one of them—thought that the fact that the Americans had that weekend stepped up their bombing of North Vietnam, and had attacked oil installations in Hanoi and Haiphong, may have had some relevance to Cousins' decision. This does not, however, appear to have weighed with him.

Others have suggested that he was naive or gullible enough to believe that he could still secure some last-minute modifications to the prices and incomes policy. Had he, perhaps, they surmised, been given some kind of assurance during that telephone call he received at Nuneaton on the eve of the election? If so, Cousins might be guilty of brinkmanship, while others might be held to have out-manœuvred him. Whatever his motives, or his arguments, he delayed his departure until the very last possible moment.

Once the decision was taken, and he was again a 'free' man, Cousins was enormously relieved. Geoffrey Goodman wrote in the *Sun*: 'He seems like a man relieved of a burden. He told me last night "I was singing at home on Tuesday for the first time for a long time."' Goodman does not tell us what Cousins was singing. Could it have been, 'For all the saints, who from their labours rest'? Or, perhaps a verse from Watts:

> Birds in their little nests agree
> And tis a shameful sight,
> When children of one family
> Fall out, and chide and fight.

The pent-up frustrations of his twenty months in the Government, his dislike of Parliament and the knowledge

L

that he had not been a conspicuous success there, no doubt contributed to his sense of release. In a highly illuminating article in the *Daily Mail*, shortly after his resignation, Cousins himself answered the question:

'Why should a trade unionist like me, dedicated by a life-time's work and ideals to strive for a Labour Government in Whitehall, walk out in its first really secure year of power?'

His action, he said, was not taken lightly, nor had it 'any basis in a desire to lead any revolt against Mr Wilson's administration'. It was the result of frustration at the way Government seemed powerless to come to grips with the crucial economic position facing the country. He agreed with his colleagues that Britain's basic problems arose because of its failure to raise production and to overcome the balance of payments problem.

> This is common ground. But from there on we have differed constantly. . . . On many occasions I have talked with the Prime Minister and with senior Cabinet colleagues, but frankly I have been getting nowhere.

He made the revealing comment:

> I have been able to establish common understanding with many of the top men in industry, yet I have failed to get across to my colleagues and to those in Whitehall who have control over our economic affairs, that a restrictive prices and incomes policy will solve nothing.

For several days during the crisis which followed his resignation Cousins was dogged by reporters and photographers. A photographer wanted to take a picture of his house—Cousins was then living in Carshalton Beeches—and was told, 'Why take a picture of the house? The house didn't resign.'

Reactions to Cousins' resignation were mixed. George Brown had 'No comment' on the night of July 3rd, but the next day he said on BBC Panorama: 'I think Mr Cousins'

arguments are wrong,' and added that he was 'a bit letting
down those chaps' who had not got much bargaining power.
Brown did not, however, think the Labour party would be
'disturbed and divided'.

George Woodcock, interviewed in the *Sunday Times*, rejected Cousins' thesis that an incomes policy would be made
unnecessary by increased productivity.

> I'm sure the people who bleat about productivity are
> genuine, but they don't quite frankly know what they are
> talking about. This is true of Frank. It is true of every-
> body who talks of this.

He also disagreed with Cousins' theory that 'trade unions
must be free at all levels to do what they like'. The unions, in
Woodcock's view, must have regard to national economic
policy.

Most of the press comment regarded Cousins' departure as
inevitable. The *Guardian*, indeed, asked, 'Why did he hang on
so long? He ought to have gone a year ago. The Government
will be stronger without him.' *The Times*, by contrast, described his resignation as 'the most politically significant since
Aneurin Bevan's in 1951' and said: 'His departure is a heavy
blow to Mr Wilson and his Government.'

At that time, as in 1956, the question everybody was asking
was: would Cousins now assume the role of leader of the
left? As in 1956, he discounted any such intentions. 'I have
no wish to become leader of the left, and I have no reason to
make me feel they want me to be their leader,' he said. 'No
one from the left has approached me and I have not approached anyone.'

At a union conference in Ireland, a few weeks after his
resignation, he was reported as saying: 'This is not Frank
Cousins coming back to lead a new campaign like a Messiah.'

Yet, as so often in his career, nobody could be quite sure of
his next move. The left-wingers would no doubt have been

glad to harness him to their tumbril and so long as he remained in Parliament this might have been feasible. But Cousins, as was shown in his CND days, had a pathological dislike of being 'used' by any group, or organisation, other than his own union. In any event, the Union soon made short shrift of any ambitions he might have nurtured to remain a Member of Parliament.

On Monday, July 4th, telegrams were sent out from Transport House summoning members of the general executive council to a special emergency meeting. The thirty-eight members assembled on the Wednesday, and met for five and a half hours. The executive accepted Cousins' return to the Union, and his reasons for resigning—not without some brotherly comments about his timing—but insisted that it was physically impossible for him to combine the House of Commons with the Union's General Secretaryship. He was told, bluntly, 'You must resign your seat at the earliest possible moment,' though in the meantime he should continue to fight the Prices and Incomes Bill from the floor of the House.

Two other events of interest happened at the July 6th meeting. The executive voted him a £500-a-year increase—a rise of 15 per cent, well above the Government's 'norm'—which brought his salary up to £3,750. He had received £8,500 as a Minister and was therefore making a considerable financial sacrifice in resigning. He was, however, expected to refund an agreed amount from his Parliamentary salary to the Union. Harry Nicholas reverted to his old position of Assistant General Secretary, though he retained a salary of £3,250, and Jack Jones stepped down to number three in the hierarchy.

The second event was when Len Forden, the Union President, agreed to vacate his seat on the TUC General Council, so as to give Cousins a clear run. It has been traditional for the TGWU to nominate a 'lay' or rank-and-file member to the General Council, and Forden, a Lancashire busman, had filled the seat since 1958. Cousins described his action as 'one of the greatest gestures ever'. A year later the executive insisted on its democratic right to nominate a lay member. Bill Jones, the veteran London busman, was named for the General Council, and this meant general post for the Union's top leadership. Harry Nicholas returned to the Labour party executive, of which he had formerly been Treasurer, and Jack Jones was left out in the cold.

Cousins was disappointed at the executive's ruling. He had told the Nuneaton party that he wanted to remain as MP and would try to persuade his executive to let him. But, as at Brighton in 1957, he was forced to bow to the democratic decision. He went up to Nuneaton the weekend after his resignation and completely won over the party's general management committee. Only two hands were raised in opposition when the Chairman proposed a vote of confidence in Cousins, backing his action in resigning from the Government, and pressing him to stay on in Parliament.

The TGWU action in instructing Frank Cousins about his Parliamentary duties and the disposal of his salary was immediately raised as a possible breach of Parliamentary privilege. Eric Lubbock, Liberal MP for Orpington, asked for the Speaker's ruling: was it right for an outside body to give orders to a Member of Parliament? Lubbock recalled the case of W. J. Brown's relations with the Civil Service Clerical Association in 1947, which had produced a resolution from the House of Commons laying down that the duty of a Member was 'to his constituents and to the country as a whole, rather than to any particular section thereof'.

Despite the furore which lasted for several days, the privilege issue was not pressed. The Speaker ruled that as the matter had not been immediately reported it was now 'out of time'.

Much the same issue flared up again a year later, when the TGWU conference at Blackpool carried a resolution indicating that the twenty-six sponsored Members of Parliament risked losing financial support unless they toed the union line in the House. Cousins said: 'We are not at all satisfied with the behaviour of some of our MPs,' and some of the delegates went a great deal farther. One declared: 'You cannot expect us to buy dog licences for dogs who bite us.' This was a reference to the Prime Minister's canine metaphor when he rebuked the Parliamentary Labour party in March and warned:

> Every dog is allowed one bite but a different view is taken of a dog that goes on biting all the time. . . . He may not get his licence renewed when it falls due.

The move to declare the TGWU resolution a breach of privilege did not materialise. Students of the British constitution were thus twice deprived of the opportunity of a debate which might have produced some interesting conclusions about the relations between trade unions and their Members of Parliament.

In the summer of 1966, however, public attention was swiftly diverted from the niceties of Parliamentary procedure by the shattering events of July 20th. On that day Harold Wilson announced in the House of Commons what one observer described as 'the harshest set of financial austerities since 1949', and what a Parliamentary wag called 'Cripps with everything'. In fact, the Wilsonian deflation, with its complete standstill on incomes, was far harsher than anything inflicted on the economy by Sir Stafford Cripps, or even by Selwyn Lloyd.

The crisis developed with bewildering rapidity and the Prime Minister himself admitted: 'Suddenly we seem to have been driven off course.' In May and June the seamen's strike and the deterioration in the balance of trade had led to a mounting lack of confidence in sterling, and to growing speculation about the possibility of devaluation. On July 5th the June reserves were published and showed a fall of £49 million. The pound had its worst day since November 1964. For some days Ministers kept up a brave façade and sought to 'play it cool'. Harold Wilson even flew to Moscow to talk with the Kremlin about peace in Vietnam. On July 14th Bank Rate was raised to 7 per cent and the Chancellor of the Exchequer announced that other measures would follow.

Behind the scenes there were frantic preparations for the Prime Minister's announcement, and bitter arguments raged within the Cabinet between the expansionists, headed by George Brown, and the axe-men, identified with the Chancellor. The Treasury, as always, won the battle. Brown, faced with the collapse of his prices and incomes policy, and the slashing of his beloved National Plan, handed in his resignation on the afternoon of Wednesday, July 20th. For nearly ten hours his friends and colleagues argued with him and pleaded with him to reconsider his decision. At midnight he withdrew it.

The deflationary package comprised a total estimated saving of £500 million. It included, on the home front, curbs on hire purchase, increased duties on alcohol, petrol and purchase tax, and cuts in public and private investment; overseas there were cuts in Government spending and the foreign travel allowance was reduced to a Crippsian level of £50 per head. The most sensational new development was the plan for a six months' standstill on all incomes and prices, to be followed by a further six months of severe restraint. 'All this is tough, and it is meant to be tough,' the Prime Minister told the nation in a TV broadcast that night.

Labour MPs who had fought their election campaigns barely four months before on a 'Let's go with Labour' expansionist platform were stunned. Was it so very different, they asked, from the Selwyn Lloyd 'Stop-Go' which Wilson had denounced so vehemently and effectively? Official spokesmen hastened to point out that spending on the social services, and investment in the development areas, had been exempted from the cuts. Yet, in some ways, the programme was a good deal more savage than that of 1961–2. Not even Selwyn Lloyd had dared to put a complete stop on pay. His 'pause' allowed for existing wage contracts to be honoured, while his 2½ per cent 'guiding light', which was to follow the pause, compared with the 'nil' norm proposed by the Labour Government.

As soon as the Prime Minister announced the plan for a universal wage freeze the TUC sent a deputation to see the Chancellor of the Exchequer and the Minister for Economic Affairs. They did not get much satisfaction from their interview, and demanded to see the Prime Minister himself. Wilson told them on July 25th that the Government had acted with great reluctance, but had no choice. The alternative, he said, would be mass unemployment. The Government, he told them bluntly, hoped for co-operation and support from the TUC—'but if we don't get it, we'll go ahead without it'.

The General Council held a long and agonising session two days later. In the end, patriotism, loyalty to the Labour party, combined with their fear of unemployment and the sense of their own impotence, prevailed. The Council issued a statement recognising that 'measures of the type and severity announced would not have been introduced by a Labour Government, unless it had been overwhelmingly convinced that they were necessary'. It therefore decided to adopt an attitude of 'reluctant acquiescence' in the standstill. Frank Cousins, though he had left the Government, had not yet returned to the TUC. He was to fight the battle in another place.

15

In and out of Parliament

Fʀᴏᴍ the time he resigned until he returned to the TUC
General Council in September 1966 Frank Cousins was primarily engaged in fighting the Prices and Incomes Bill on the
floor of the House of Commons. He failed to enlist the support of more than a handful of trade union MPs, even among
those who were sponsored by his own union. The fact that the
overwhelming majority of the TGWU-sponsored MPs were
drawn from the ranks of teachers, lawyers and other profes-
sions, rather than from those of manual workers, may have
had some bearing on their attitude.

Nevertheless, Cousins' Parliamentary performances as a
back-bencher impressed even the most cynical observers.
Where he had been rigid and pompous he became relaxed
and conversational, and began to make the kind of speeches
he himself, and not his permanent officials, wanted. On July
14th, making his 'maiden' speech from the back benches, he
spoke for about half an hour, and elaborated his reasons for
resigning.

> I have been told I ought not to worry about the Bill.
> After all, they said, it is not such a bad Bill and everybody
> knows it won't work. I was told it was not a big enough
> thing for me to resign on. How cynical can you get? How
> unrelated to the realities of life? This problem is not going
> to be solved in here.

The Commons, unused to such phraseology, listened in-
tently and with a great deal of sympathy. A Labour front-
bencher later told me: 'It was electrifying. He brought a

breath of fresh air into Westminster. It was the authentic voice of the workers, who are, dammit, the people we are supposed to represent.'

The Times Parliamentary correspondent noted:

> This was a new Mr Cousins. A translation to the back benches had almost, but not quite, turned Mr Cousins into a House of Commons man. . . . He struck out on his own through country where the union is king, the employer his consort and the politician a mere irrelevance.

A few weeks later Cousins was appointed to Standing Committee B on the Bill. The Committee consisted of fourteen Labour MPs and ten Conservatives and met under the chairmanship of Harold Lever. It held seven sessions between July 26th and August 4th, and two of these lasted all night. Cousins complained about the time-table. 'Are we to be wearied into submission?' he asked. He proposed some nineteen separate amendments to the Bill and fought it, line by line, clause by clause, for the most part single-handed.

He missed the first session—he was attending a union function in Bristol—and his absence led one Tory MP to ask: 'Where is Mr Cousins? Without him, it is like *Hamlet* without the Ghost' [*sic*]. Norman St John-Stevas suggested that Cousins was Lady Macbeth, come armed with daggers to slay the Bill. Cousins himself invoked 'Much ado about nothing' and William Rodgers, Under-Secretary for the Department of Economic Affairs, capped it with a reference to the Midsummer Night's Dream turning into a Winter's Tale. All this Shakespeareana perhaps provided some light relief but it did not affect the bitterness of the drama that was played out in committee room number 11. Cousins made a blanket condemnation of the Bill:

> It is a bad Bill and I shall continue to say it is a bad Bill. It is a move to make the trade union movement an adjunct of the Government. I don't think you can have free trade

unions in a social democratic society when the intention of
the Bill is to tell the unions what they can and cannot do.

His main objections, which he deployed during the committee stage—and in subsequent speeches and articles—can
be conveniently summarised:

1. The answer to Britain's economic problems is not
deflation and wage restraint, but higher production and increased industrial investment and modernisation.

2. It is ridiculous to put a stop to productivity bargaining.

3. Britain is a low wage economy compared with many of
its overseas competitors.

4. The Bill constitutes intervention in free collective bargaining; it is totalitarian and places a dangerous weapon in
the hands of future Governments.

5. It will create bad labour relations, discourage improvements in productivity and lead to lack of co-operation within
industry.

6. It is unworkable.

On several occasions he found himself voting with the
Conservatives, but he was nettled at the suggestion that he
was helping the Opposition. 'I am not supporting the Conservatives—I am opposing the Bill,' he declared angrily, just
before he stalked out of the Committee in dudgeon at 4 a.m.
on August 5th.

The critics failed in their bid to alter the Bill, which duly
became law on August 12th. Part IV, which gave the Government powers to enforce the standstill, remained in abeyance
until October 5th, when it was decided to activate it. The
decision, reached during the Labour party conference at
Brighton, was touched off by the refusal of the Newspaper
Proprietors' Association to delay paying a cost-of-living increase to print workers. The NPA argued that a court
judgment given against Thorn Electrical Industries to a member of Clive Jenkins' union, ASSET, upholding his entitle-

ment to a wage contract negotiated before July 20th, left
them no alternative. Many people in the Labour party saw
behind this move the sinister hand of the press barons,
motivated by their desire to embarrass the Labour Government.

The Cabinet held an emergency meeting in the Prime
Minister's suite in the Grand Hotel and reached their decision
unanimously. While three Ministers were winging their way
from Brighton to Balmoral to seek the Queen's assent to the
Order, a gloomy Chancellor told conference delegates: 'Those
who wanted to force the Government to use compulsion have
had their way.'

The Order was laid before Parliament on October 25th,
and at least twenty-eight MPs abstained in defiance of a three-
line Whip. Cousins was one of them. His abstention was held
to fall within the category of 'a deeply held and conscientious
conviction'.

Eleven days later, November 5th, Cousins announced his
decision to resign as member of Parliament for Nuneaton.

Before turning to his campaign outside the Commons
against the prices and incomes policy it is perhaps worth
taking a final look at him as a Parliamentarian. The date of
his announcement was highly symbolic, because, like Guy
Fawkes, he had demonstrated his contempt for Parliament,
though in a rather less explosive manner. He told reporters:

> I have no regrets about leaving the House. I think the
> House wastes a lot of time. The House bores and irritates
> me.

To him, the House was a 'silly place', which did not tackle
the serious subjects, or probe into things that were important,
but was concerned with trivialities. He was irked by the
archaic procedures and thought, for example, that for a busy
and overworked Minister to have to sit up till 11.30 p.m.,
just so that he could nod his assent, was the negation of good

management. He spent as little time as he could in the Palace. An assiduous reporter on the *Daily Telegraph* dug out his division record over a period—out of 144 divisions he had voted in 24; he was paired in 60 and absent, unpaired, in another 60.

A sympathetic colleague commented: 'His trade union training had been strong and astringent, but it did not equip him for politics. He thought the House was full of humbug and used to call it a "temple of hypocrisy" '.

This attitude, in one who had come to Westminster the easy way via a safe seat, was not calculated to endear him to Members who had struggled to get themselves elected for marginal constituencies. I asked a leading left-wing MP: 'Are you sorry that Frank is leaving the House?' 'No,' he replied tersely. Cousins was an awkward element; he held himself aloof from political gossip and did not mix much in the smoking-room or tea bars. He carried his antipathy to almost ludicrous lengths. A very junior TUC official, on his way to a meeting in the House one evening, met Cousins in the central lobby. He did not know that Cousins would even recognise him and was amazed when he strode across, shook him warmly by the hand and exclaimed: 'My goodness, it's nice to see a trade union face after all these politicians!' Cousins shied very clear of the lobby correspondents, making only exceptions for those who, like Ian Aitken of the *Guardian*, had at one time been industrial correspondents, and therefore knew about the world that mattered.

The Times political correspondent commented that Cousins' departure marked 'the final failure of a governmental and political experiment that had some importance'. Cousins had shown that Parliament was 'not a place into which an established man of power and influence can be successfully introduced from the outside to cross-fertilise Cabinets and the House with ideas and methods current in big industry and big unions'.

'Why is the Commons a place where lawyers, teachers, journalists, PR men and rank-and-file trade unionists in abundance can make a contented career, while the occasional tycoon from either side of industry is a sad, frustrated misfit, who quickly returns to the world he knows?' he asked.

Cousins was indeed happy to return to his own world, the world of direct speech and action, where, in his mind, real power lies. He might well have agreed with Aneurin Bevan, who was for so long baffled in his search for power. Bevan told the House of Commons in 1943 how, as a small boy, he had decided:

'The place to get to is the Council. That's where power lies. I got on to the Council. I discovered when I got there that power had been there, but it had just gone.' So he worked to get on the County Council. 'I got there, but it had gone from there too. Then I found it had come up here [to the House of Commons]. So I followed it and sure enough I found that it had been here but I just saw its coat-tails round the corner. The ordinary man in Great Britain has been spending his life for the last couple of generations in this will-o'-the-wisp pursuit of power, trying to get his hands on the levers of big policy, and trying to find out where it is, and how it was that his life was shaped for him by somebody else.'

Cousins was as genuinely sorry to leave Nuneaton as the local party was to see him go. 'This is probably the saddest moment I have had for a long time,' he said, as he paid his farewell visit to the constituency.

Up to the last minute the local party had tried to persuade him to stay on, and even sent a three-man deputation to the Union's executive meeting in September. After a close vote the executive gave the Nuneaton party permission to address the meeting and state their case. The three men waited expectantly in Cousins' room upstairs while the executive argued on and on in the council chamber. Cousins eventually came to tell them that the union had reaffirmed its earlier decision, and that he could not undertake the two jobs. They returned, somewhat crestfallen, to Nuneaton.

The local people liked him, once they had got over their resentment at the way in which their former Member, Frank Bowles, had been 'kicked upstairs' to make room for him. 'Greater love for his constituents hath no man than he gives up his seat for his cousins,' quipped Frank Bowles, as he made his way to the House of Lords.

'Mr Cousins is a jolly good constituency MP,' said the chairman of his constituency party, Mr Herbert Knight. He had, by all accounts, been extremely conscientious, visiting his constituents as often as he could and taking up their cases. During the 1966 election, a heckler at a market-place meeting declared that Cousins would not be seen in Nuneaton after polling day. 'You liar!' Nance Cousins shouted at him. 'Frank has been more times in his constituency than most MPs and certainly more than the Tory candidate.' The general feeling in Nuneaton was that he could not both be their Member and the General Secretary of his union. One veteran Labour supporter commented: 'There is a principle in the Labour party—one dog, one bone.'

Cousins finally and officially resigned from the House of Commons on December 5th, when he was appointed 'steward and bailiff of the Manor of Northstead' (technically an office of profit under the Crown). 'In the nick of time,' commented a member of his union executive, which was due to meet that very day. There might, he said, have been ructions if Cousins had prolonged his Membership of Parliament, and violated the 'one dog, one bone' principle.

Even while still a MP Cousins had carried on his vigorous campaign against the Prices and Incomes Bill, on the different, but, to him, more familiar battleground of the trade union movement. At the TUC at Blackpool in September he moved a resolution rejecting the whole concept of the pay freeze and the prices and incomes policy. He elaborated most of the arguments he had used in the House of Commons, but concentrated primarily on the threat to the trade unions. His theme was:

> You cannot have a social democracy and at the same time control by legislation the activity of a free trade union movement which is an essential part of that social democracy.

Cousins spoke well and to the point, but his reception did not compare with the one he had received ten years earlier at Brighton, when he condemned the Tory policy of wage restraint. On that occasion, he had been given a rapturous ovation. This time, his speech fell very flat. There were groans and an audible cry of 'Bighead', when he declared this was not a question of personalities or of 'Harold Wilson versus Frank Cousins'.

The Prime Minister, at his own request, had addressed the Congress on the opening day, and the majority of delegates rose to applaud him when he had finished his speech. Cousins remained seated and so did most of his union delegation. But at least one member stood up and, unfortunately for him, was included in the picture of Cousins taken by a press photographer. Next day he was reprimanded by Cousins for 'breaking the ranks'. Since he has left the Union to join the Prices and Incomes Board and was, in any case, identifiable from the picture, there seems no harm now in saying that this was Ron Mathias, South Wales regional secretary of the TGWU, one of the most consistent critics of Cousins' policy.

(Incidentally, it is a curious feature of present-day Labour conferences that popularity is gauged by the numbers that stand, and those who do not. At one conference in the 1950s it was calculated by William Barkley, in the *Daily Express*, according to the length of the applause measured by his stopwatch.)

Cousins was scathing about the Prime Minister's speech:

I did not agree with the Government policy when I left and I do not agree with it now. Nothing the Prime Minister has said will make me change my mind.

He did not, however, succeed in swinging the Trades Union Congress to his way of thinking, though he found an unexpected ally in NALGO, the local government white-collar workers' union, noted for its respectability and its past reluctance to associate with the TUC. Delegates were impressed by the speech of Vic Feather, standing in for George Woodcock who was in hospital after a heart attack, and by the argument of Sir Harry Douglass, the steel union leader: 'We cannot have a voluntary system for the simple reason that we do not have enough volunteers.'

The General Council's attitude of 'reluctant acquiescence' in the Government's economic policy was endorsed, but only by the narrow margin of 344,000. The Cousins resolution was defeated by 5,037,000 votes to 3,903,000, a majority of 1,134,000.

A month later the whole proceedings were repeated at the Labour party conference at Brighton, but the support for the Government was decisive and clear-cut. The official policy was accepted by 3,836,000 votes to 2,515,000 and most of the constituency delegates appeared to support the platform. Cousins moved an omnibus resolution protesting against the freeze and the threat of anti-trade union legislation. He said:

We in the T and G regard this as a tragic day for principles and for commonsense. We regard this as a day which we shall live very seriously to regret when the Government for the first time tells us that a Labour administration believes that the way to solve our economic problems is to use the instrument of the Conservatives against the trade union movement.

Cousins was loudly applauded while he was speaking, and when he left the rostrum. But, as at the TUC, he could not resist the introduction of the third person singular.

M

> This is not a challenge from Frank Cousins and the
> T and GWU to anyone else ...

His resolution was defeated by 3,925,000 votes to 2,471,000. Cousins, however, could take comfort in the defeat of the National Executive in two resolutions which his union sponsored. One, which he moved, calling for a substantial cut in defence expenditure and an end to the East of Suez policy, was carried by 538,000 votes. The other, moved by Harry Nicholas, urged the introduction of short-time working as an alternative to unemployment. This was carried by 152,000 votes, despite an impassioned appeal for its rejection by Ray Gunter.

Harold Wilson was later asked what the Government would do about this defeat on an important issue of economic policy. 'Govern,' he growled. Like Hugh Gaitskell six years before, he made it clear that the leadership would not let itself be dictated to by the party conference. Yet this was the very issue on which he himself had challenged Gaitskell for the leadership in 1960.

Cousins may not have carried the delegates all the way with him in the Rank Ice Palace where the conference was held. He certainly captured the imagination and enthusiasm of the audience at a packed rally called by the left-wing paper *Tribune* at the Corn Exchange. It was his first appearance on a *Tribune* platform, and he was given a film star's reception. He laid down the terms on which he would co-operate:

> I will work for the Government, with the Government and for the members of my union for the general good of the working-class community of which I am proud to be a member. I will not work under the Government. We want to be partners. We do not intend to be servants.

Though this was good rousing stuff and though he publicly associated himself with *Tribune*, he was still far from declaring himself as the potential head of a new left-wing alignment.

By this time, Cousins had returned to the TUC fold and had secured election to its key committees. His critics were delighted when he polled fewer votes in the ballot for the General Council than his number two, Harry Nicholas, and said gleefully: 'That will take him down a peg or two.' The *Guardian* struck a rather waspish note:

> Who loves Cousins now? Big Frank has diminished over the last few weeks, is still diminishing and shows every sign of shrinking further.

Some of his colleagues noted that he seemed more restrained than in the past. They were greatly surprised when, without demur, he took his place as a newcomer at the 'minnows' end' of the horseshoe table in the TUC boardroom, instead of claiming the seniority to which he would have been entitled, but for his broken service. Incidentally, he missed the chance of becoming TUC Chairman, which would have come to him, under the seniority rule, in 1969. Cousins did not mind where he sat, so long as his voice could carry, and he was never unduly concerned about the trappings of office.

Within his own union there were mixed reactions to his return. Many of his national officials disapproved of his opposition to the Labour Government's policy, but were constitutionally debarred from making their views known. According to one estimate, about a third of the members of the Executive Council were disturbed about the Union's course, but, as so often, were inhibited from expressing their opposition. As for the rank and file, there has been little opportunity to gauge their opinions. Among the more militant sections, such as busmen, dockers and Midlands car workers, there was support for the toughest possible line, while union members who were involved in productivity bargaining resented Government policy.

In my own enquiries in some of the more remote country

areas, where the branches are of a mixed, or general nature, I found considerable concern that the Union had not been loyal to the Government it had done so much to help elect. There was very little sympathy for the Midlands car workers, who were the first victims of the freeze.

The great British public, to judge from the evidence of opinion polls, supported the Government against Cousins. After he had resigned the question was asked in the Gallup Poll (published in the *Daily Telegraph*): 'Would you like to see Cousins leading a left-wing group of the Labour party?' The replies were: 'No' 53 per cent, 'Yes' 13 per cent, and 'Don't know' 34 per cent. A poll conducted among trade unionists on the eve of the September TUC showed that 62 per cent accepted the freeze, compared with 26 per cent against, and 12 per cent 'don't knows'.

The extent to which the nation, and the Labour movement, tolerated the wages standstill was a surprise even to the most Walter Mittyish members of the Government. The very completeness of the stop, and the fact that it gave no opportunity for evasion or queue-jumping, appealed to the British sense of fair play. Just how effective the standstill proved is shown in the official statistics. The wage plateau was held—the Ministry of Labour's index of wage rates rose from 154.5 to 154.6 between July and December. Prices rose rather more, as a result of the selective employment tax, but at a lower rate than in the preceeding year. The wave of industrial unrest, which many had predicted, did not materialise. During the six months of the standstill period 195,000 workers were involved in stoppages which cost 606,000 working days, the bulk of these being in the motor-car industry. In the comparable period of 1965 the figures were 324,000 workers and a loss of 915,000 working days. There was, however, a sharp set-back in production, and the unemployment figure crept up to near the half-million mark. The Government could, and did, claim that freeze and squeeze combined were having their effect in steadying the economy and restoring confidence in the pound. The President of the Board of Trade, Douglas Jay, declared: 'The July measures appear to be having their intended effect in improving the trade balance and strengthening sterling.'

From this picture it might be concluded that Frank Cousins' campaign against the Government's prices and incomes policy had been an utter failure. It certainly failed in the short term, and there was no mass revolt by trade unionists, even among those who belonged to the Transport Union. But, as we shall see in the next chapter, a very different atmosphere developed as the Government began to work out its plans for the period after the standstill. There was a distinct veering of trade union opinion in Cousins' direction, and the TUC moved from its earlier attitude of 'reluctant acquiescence' to one of 'Don't push us too far'.

16

All power to the TUC

T HE most significant moment at the Trades Union Congress at Blackpool in September 1966 was when Frank Cousins half turned away from the audience and, waving his hand in the direction of the General Council on the platform, declared:

> If the trade unions themselves are going to surrender their authority, I suggest they will want to surrender it to this body here and not to a Government.

It was, some said, one of the most dramatic conversions since St Paul's journey to Damascus. The TGWU, both under Deakin and Cousins, had steadily resisted the idea that individual unions should surrender any authority to the General Council. It was largely owing to their implacable opposition that the ideas of men like Charles Geddes and Alan Birch for arming the TUC with an effective general staff had foundered. The late Bryn Roberts, leader of the Public Employees' Union, who had been regarded by Deakin as a sort of trade union Dick Turpin, out to waylay county roadmen, labourers and hospital orderlies who were the 'natural' members of the TGWU, had persistently but vainly preached the doctrine of centralisation, and the vesting of real power in the General Council. 'The General Council is supposed to be a spearhead for the movement,' he once said. 'As a spearhead, it's about as blunt as a bus.'

In 1957 Cousins told the TUC that only one body was competent to tell his union how to run its business, and that was its own general executive council. In 1963 he was decidedly lukewarm about the proposals for giving the TUC more central authority, which George Woodcock had passionately advocated. As recently as 1965, the TGWU representatives had poured scorn on the TUC plan for wage-vetting machinery, and in the next few months sent in such a flood of claims to be examined that the pipeline was almost completely jammed.

Cousins' change of front was a major factor in the TUC's decision to develop its own incomes policy in the autumn of 1966. It helped stiffen the unions' determination to keep the Government out of the field of collective bargaining.

In the early days of the Labour Government there had been a broad consensus of opinion in favour of the prices and incomes policy and the TGWU had been almost alone in standing outside. As late as September 1966 the TUC was still committed, albeit reluctantly, to supporting Government policy. But the Transport Union found itself in a growing minority which eventually became the majority. Several factors contributed to the change in the unions' attitude. The most potent force was the rise in unemployment.

Union leaders had accepted the standstill on the Prime Minister's assurance that it was the only alternative to mass unemployment, but it seemed to them, as they studied the mounting monthly figures that they were getting the worst of both worlds—the freeze *and* unemployment. Between July and October the number of unemployed leaped by over 170,000 to 437,000, and by New Year 1967 it had reached 600,000, or 2.6 per cent of the total number of workers. Deeply alarmed at the trend, the General Council urged the Government to take the brakes off. Both the Prime Minister and the Chancellor refused to be 'stampeded' into premature reflation. 'There can be no general let-up until the economy is really sound and we are paying our way,' Mr Wilson said on November 12th.

Two personalities also had a catalytic effect on events. George Woodcock had missed the Congress in September through illness, but he returned in late October, reinvigorated after a Mexican convalescence, to lead the battle against Government interference. 'Like the hero in a Western, riding over the border to defend the cowed citizens of some township terrorised by a marauding gang of cattle rustlers, he returned hotfoot from Mexico to instil the spirit of resistance into the TUC,' was the *New Statesman*'s picturesque analogy.

The other change was the substitution of Michael Stewart, the Foreign Secretary, for George Brown as Minister for Economic Affairs, when the two swapped jobs in late September. Cousins was scathing about the change. 'Nobody could make that policy work,' he said. Most trade union leaders missed the earthy effervescence of George Brown and suspected the somewhat academic approach of his successor.

The Prime Minister had given the TUC an assurance in September: 'We do not seek as a long-term policy to destroy the machinery of collective bargaining. That is a pledge I give you.' But there was evidence of a growing school of thought within Government circles in favour of retaining some permanent powers over prices and incomes. In contrast to the *laissez-faire* views of Enoch Powell and other right-wing Tories, many former left-wing Ministers regarded wages planning as an important instrument for the achievement of Socialism. A speech by Richard Crossman the weekend after the Trades Union Congress, warning that there could be no return to the pre-July 20th position, alarmed many union leaders. The *New Statesman* hailed the prices and incomes policy as a step 'on the long arduous road which could eventually promote Socialism in this country'. A remark by William Rodgers, then Parliamentary Secretary at the Department of Economic Affairs, at a *Guardian* 'Teach-in' in late October, added fuel to the flames. He said:

If, at the end of the day, the Government has to go it alone, it will have to use whatever means may be appropriate to enforce an effective policy. The Government must govern and failure to agree on the implementation of a policy which the country both needs and wants could not mean its abandonment.

The thesis advanced by Aubrey Jones, Chairman of the Prices and Incomes Board, before the Royal Commission on Trade Unions was visibly gaining support. He said that the state of the economy was 'too precarious' to permit a return to the sort of voluntary arrangements obtaining before July 20th. He elaborated his views in a round-table discussion 'Beyond the Freeze' in November. His opposite numbers were Lord Robens and Frank Cousins, both looking rather shaggy and larger than life, compared with his own slim, precise figure.

Aubrey Jones said that the present employer-union situation was reminiscent of the Middle Ages. 'You have in effect two sets of feudal barons. We can't disband the barons—there they are in front of us, Frank and Alf, both of them barons.' The only way of dealing with them, he suggested, was to call into being a 'countervailing force' in the form of a tribunal to which the barons would be accountable. Such a tribunal could decide on the pros and cons of increases in wages and prices and would, in effect, operate the prices and incomes policy. Cousins could barely contain himself. He kept up a running comment of 'Nonsense . . . utter nonsense' and twice accused Aubrey Jones of making 'extraordinary' statements.

Trade unionists may not have liked it, but the idea that the consumer needed to be protected against the producers, on both sides of industry, was fairly popular with the general public.

The introduction of the Factory Acts and the establishment by Winston Churchill in 1909 of Trade Boards to

protect sweated workers against exploitation were bitterly opposed by the employers as the thin end of the wedge of State
intervention in industry. For the Government to take an
interest in the field of collective bargaining might be held by
some to be a logical development of this process. But 'Hands
off collective bargaining' has become a rallying cry for the
trade union movement.

This opposition can only be understood in the light of trade
union history and traditions. It is therefore perhaps appropriate, on the eve of the TUC centenary, to recall the challeng-
ing question put by George Woodcock in 1960. 'What are we
here for?' he asked. He was speaking in the comparatively
narrow context of trade union structure, but he raised the
wider issues of the unions' place in modern society and
touched off a debate which was to rage furiously throughout
the first half of the decade, and culminate in the appointment
of a Royal Commission in 1965.

In its evidence before the Royal Commission, the TUC
sought to answer Woodcock's question. It harked back to the
Webbs' definition of a union 'as a continuous association of
wage-earners for the purpose of improving the conditions of
their working lives'. Of all union objectives, 'improved wages
and terms of employment stands at the top' and collective
bargaining was the accepted means of achieving this aim.
The Government's role should be strictly limited to spheres
where trade union organisation was too weak to develop free
collective bargaining and safeguard the interests of the
workers. 'No State, however benevolent, can perform the
function of trade unions in enabling workpeople themselves
to decide how their interests can best be safeguarded.'

The TUC evidence was savaged by most newspapers; it
was called 'vague', 'complacent', 'negative' and 'a damp
squib'. But Woodcock defended it and described it as 'an
impressive statement of what trade unionism is about'. The
TUC definition of the purpose of the unions was four-square

with Cousins' own philosophy. In the TGWU evidence to the Commission, an almost identical phrase appeared:

> We believe that the primary function of trade unions is to maintain and improve the condition of their members' working lives by effective collective bargaining.

The TUC told the Royal Commission that it believed in an incomes policy, but that it must be on a voluntary basis, and without Government interference.

> The General Council . . . are convinced that if a way forward is to be found, it will be through the strengthening of the TUC's role in examining and influencing the pattern of claims and settlements, and not through intervention by Government in the process of collective bargaining.

The first positive step in the 'do it yourself' direction by the TUC was a decision in October 1966 to revive its wage-vetting machinery which had been in cold storage since July 20th. The economic committee met, unprecedently, on a Sunday and spent the whole day, with a brief break for coffee and sandwiches, thrashing out an alternative policy to the Government's. Members of the committee noted the similarity of Woodcock's and Cousins' thinking, and their utter determination to keep the Government out.

Cousins threw out what his friends regarded as a 'life-line' but some resented as a publicity stunt. The so-called 'Cousins Plan', which he had launched a few days earlier at a union rally, provided for the setting up of two-tier negotiating machinery very much on the Swedish pattern. According to this plan, the TUC and the Confederation of British Industries would agree a national minimum wage for adult workers —Cousins' own target was £15 a week—and reach national agreements on hours, holidays and fringe benefits. At lower level there would be plant and company bargaining, concentrating on productivity, incentives and local issues. Cousins argued that his scheme would get rid of the present 'time-

consuming, repetitious, annual scramble' and provide a uni-
fied approach; it would be an extension and modernisation
of collective bargaining; by freeing union officials of many
routine chores, it would enable them to concentrate on the
really vital business of productivity bargaining at shop-floor
level.   In words not unlike Lenin's famous battle-cry, he
called for 'All Power to the TUC'. His plan, he said,

> would bring the TUC itself into the centre of normal trade
> union activity, a role it has always lacked. This would of
> course mean the transfer of some functions from the indi-
> vidual unions and a build-up of central organisation, but it
> is felt that the movement is ready to take this step forward.

This was indeed a remarkable declaration from a man
who, until very recently, had been one of the most jealous
guardians of the rights and prerogatives of individual
unions.

The employers, not surprisingly, were not taken with the
notion of a national minimum wage of £15—some said it
would add £1,500 million a year to industry's labour costs—
but they liked the idea of closer working with the TUC. Both
sides of industry firmly grounded a kite which was being
flown from Whitehall, very much on the Aubrey Jones line,
that there should be some permanent tripartite prices and
incomes machinery, on which Government, employers and
unions would be represented. It would be a sort of 'Neddy'
for incomes and prices. The employers and the TUC did not
want a chaperon to sit in on their talks, and the CBI direc-
tor-general John Davies warned of a 'pattern of insidious
encroachment' by the Government into the affairs of
industry.

As a result of the freeze and the threat of permanent
Government intervention, employers and union leaders were
drawn more closely together than at any time since the
abortive Mond-Turner talks of 1928. They planned to hold

regular monthly meetings, six a side, to discuss common industrial problems in an informal atmosphere without, as John Davies put it, 'the feeling that we were constantly subject to comment, disagreement and correction by the Government'. The first of these meetings took place in January 1967.

It is strange to compare the lack of interest in this get-together with the uproar which greeted the announcement of the Mond-Turner talks, which were equally designed to improve industrial relations. Cousins, who was one of the TUC team, would no doubt, if challenged, have recalled Bevin's defence of his decision to join in talks with the employers:

> I am no more in alliance with them than I am in alliance with the dock owners or anybody else whom I have to fight every day. Is the strike the only way to fight? Cannot we fight by discussion, as well as starvation? Cannot we fight by intelligence?

The first serious rift between the Government and the TUC developed in late November when the Government published in a White Paper the criteria for the period of severe restraint, due to follow the standstill in January 1967. This stipulated a zero norm for the annual rate of increases in money incomes and only allowed exceptions (most of which would be referred to the Aubrey Jones Board) in the case of very low-paid workers or 'genuine' productivity agreements.

Cousins was furious. 'We are facing what amounts to another six months of freeze, with all the anomalies, injustices and barriers to economic progress which have been with us since July 20th,' he said. The TUC General Council agreed with him, and at its November meeting decided that it would not be bound either by the criteria, or the Government's interpretation of them. Instead, it decided to strengthen its own machinery and to issue annual reports on the economic situation.

> It will be a trade union view of the situation and its re-
> quirements, presented by trade unionists to trade unionists
> ... This step will in itself constitute a significant advance
> towards a co-ordinated trade union incomes policy.

A great debate then began, which was to dominate the
political scene throughout the early months of 1967: what
would happen after July/August, when the period of severe
restraint had ended and Part IV (providing compulsory
powers) had lapsed?

It would be tedious in the extreme to chronicle the endless
series of meetings which took place between Michael Stewart
and the employers' and TUC leaders. They continued almost
without interruption and seemed to be getting increasingly
bogged down in almost theological obscurity. There appeared
towards the end of February to be four alternative courses
open to the Government.

1. To let the CBI and the TUC return to their own free
collective bargaining and drop all idea of compulsory powers.
(This was the Cousins' line.)

2. To give the TUC and the CBI a chance to operate self-
discipline and allow a trial period to see whether the voluntary system could operate effectively,

3. To maintain Government control by strengthening
Part II of the Act, to enable the Government to delay increases, or

4. To continue with the operation of Part IV, the most
punitive section of the Act.

The alternatives 1 and 4 were ruled out by most Ministers
as impracticable. The clash came between the advocates of the
second and third courses, who were inevitably divided into
'doves' and 'hawks'. The principal 'dove' was Ray Gunter
who, as a former trade union leader and the man who had to
'carry the can' as Minister of Labour, realised the full implications for the delicately balanced mechanism of industrial
relations of continued compulsion. Other Ministers, includ-

ing Michael Stewart and James Callaghan, felt that previous experience of the TUC's voluntary control did not augur well for the succes of any future experiment.

The final decision was clearly one for the Prime Minister who, while his Ministers were toing and froing between Whitehall and Congress House, was himself toing and froing between the capitals of Europe. The Prime Minister, however, made it clear, at a speech in Swansea on February 3rd that there could be no return to the pre-July situation. 'The price of freedom from crisis, from stop-go, is the abandonment of a free-for-all in incomes,' he said. The Government was still determined to curb inflation and maintain confidence in the pound at all costs. Public opinion had supported Wilson so far and many voters probably approved of a 'get tough with the unions' line. But there had been ominous rumblings of discontent as trade unionists threatened to contract out of paying the political levy or withdraw support in other ways. The unions had contributed some £330,000 towards the 1966 general election, but although they had paid the piper, they seemed further away from calling the tune than at any time in the history of the Labour movement.

The crucial question in the spring of 1967 was whether what might be loosely called the 'Woodcock-Cousins' line of 'Hands off the TUC' would prevail over the views of traditional Labour loyalists, who tended to support the Government whatever it did. Cousins himself threatened that if the Government persisted in plans to maintain compulsory powers, he and his union would boycott the TUC's voluntary incomes policy. He wrote in the *Sunday Express* on February 19th:

> If the Government insists on retaining a veto on pay claims, it could sabotage right at the beginning an important initiative by the TUC which is moving towards a voluntary plan on wages. . . . This could be a valuable, if quiet, revolution. But I am quite certain that most mem-

bers of my union will see no point in supporting a TUC voluntary plan for wages, if this is to be operated under the threat of Government coercion.

He did not carry out his threat of non-co-operation when the conference of trade union executives met on March 2nd to decide their future policy. More than 1,500 union officials turned up to the Central Hall, Westminster; it was the biggest attendance ever recorded at such a conference. The issue before them: should individual unions agree to surrender more authority to the TUC?

George Woodcock, in a long speech, put it bluntly: 'We cannot operate without genuine authority. We want not a mere majority vote here, but real authority.' It was the opportunity for the TUC to do its 'real job' of looking after the interests of working people over a broad front. The TUC plan he described as 'the most fruitful set of proposals that has ever come from any trade union movement in any country at any time'.

The leaders of all the major, and many of the minor, unions, pledged their support for the TUC policy. There were only two vocal opponents—Jim Mortimer, of the engineering draughtsmen and that indefatigable opponent of the freeze, Clive Jenkins (Association of Supervisory Staffs and Technicians). Jenkins accused the unions of being frightened to fight for higher wages and said they were 'about as aggressive as hamsters'.

For the first time for several years, the Transport Union's vote was cast with the majority, but not without some argument. The night before, at an executive meeting, Bill Jones had called for a rejection of the TUC plan. He implied that Cousins was being taken for a ride, and his freedom of action would be limited. It was all very well for the TUC to talk about wages, but what could it do about prices? Despite his eloquence, Jones was outvoted by a substantial majority.

Cousins spoke briefly in support of the TUC proposals.

'We should say "Away with legislation". We have had enough of it,' he declared. The Government was 'probably the best Government we have had in this country' but it had made mistakes in its attitude towards the unions.

> We are not a body to be told what the Government wants us to do. We are not the agents and instruments of the Government. We refuse to be this to any Government.

Later that evening, on an ITV programme, he expressed his readiness to wear a martyr's crown and go to prison, if action by the Government or by a 'red-robed Judge' should lead to injustice.

The massive majority cast in favour of the General Council —7,604,000 votes to 963,000—delighted George Woodcock. It seemed that, at long last, his dream of a centralised and effective trade union machine was about to be realised.

Up to this point, the Woodcock-Cousins alliance stood firm, and the two men were completely at one on the central theme of the TUC policy. But there was a subtle change in their relative positions. In the past Woodcock had often been embarrassed by Cousins' insistence on public declarations of union support for the Labour party. Now, it was Woodcock who gave the assurance that he had no wish to 'browbeat' the Government. 'I want to work with the Government,' he said. Cousins, by contrast, saw the issue as 'very much an argument between the TUC and the Government's policy' and chided Woodcock for not being as forceful as he had been 'in other places', when the TUC had met Ministers for private talks.

The vote of the March 2nd conference was generally hailed as a 'triumph' for Woodcock. In a sense, it was also a triumph for Cousins. He could claim with some justification that his long fight against wage restraint and Government intervention had borne fruit and that the trade union movement was at last getting in step with him—or he with it.

N

17

Full circle

Less than a year after the Labour party's sweeping victory at the polls the tide of opinion began to turn against the Government. It was not so much a positive turn to the Tories as a steady seepage of support. The lead enjoyed by Labour in the Gallup Poll began to dwindle and for the first time the Prime Minister, who had for so long basked in the sunshine of popular esteem, found his personal rating falling. The picture of firm and purposive Government which had been conveyed during the earlier days changed to an impression of dither, and failure to come to grips with the rapidly developing crises in home and foreign affairs.

The Party Whips could no longer pull out the loyalty stops and rely on a precarious majority to keep the rebels under control. The left-wingers were able uninhibitedly to abstain or even oppose, in the comfortable knowledge that, while their actions might embarrass the Government, they would not bring it down.

In the 1950s the argument had been about personalities and leadership. This was not the case in the 1960s. Wilson still enjoyed undisputed authority and would certainly have been re-elected had there been a contest. The Left found a standard-bearer in Michael Foot, who decided to run for the party treasurership against James Callaghan. But there was no evidence that Foot would have the temerity to stand for the top job.

Wilson came under very much the same kind of pressures as Attlee had been under from right-wing loyalists, to stamp out incipient rebellion and enforce party discipline. But despite his stern warning to the Parliamentary party about the withdrawal of their licences, the left-wing showed no signs of being chastened. The rebels kept up their opposition to Government policy on Vietnam and defence, and to the prices and incomes policy. Many MPs voted against the decision to apply for membership of the Common Market and seven Parliamentary private secretaries, who were among the abstainers, were dismissed. Two were later reinstated.

The rebels were let off with a gentle rebuke when Parliament reassembled after the Whitsun recess. This was because a more tolerant regime had been ushered in, with the appointment of John Silkin as Chief Whip and Richard Crossman as Leader of the House. Another sign of the trend towards tolerance was the replacement by Douglas Houghton of the veteran disciplinarian Manny Shinwell as Chairman of the Parliamentary party. Houghton, a former member of the TUC General Council, and a man of sagacity and persuasiveness, had been Minister without Portfolio since October 1964, charged with bringing the Beveridge social security scheme up to date.

One day, early in the New Year of 1967, he was summoned to No. 10 Downing Street. He fully expected this would be to discuss the progress of a Cabinet working party on social services, which had been set up just before Christmas. To his consternation, he found that the object of the interview was to give him the sack. 'Sorry, Douglas, you're too old,' he was told. Patrick Gordon-Walker was appointed Minister without Portfolio in his stead. He was 61, against Houghton's 68. Many trade unionists saw in this change confirmation of their fears that the 'intellectuals' were prevailing over those with trade union backgrounds.

The first public test of the Government's popularity came in the spring of 1967, with the elections for the County Councils including Greater London. Labour suffered humiliating losses in the Counties and lost London which it had held for thirty-three years. It did even worse in the borough council elections in May, when it lost 616 seats and the Tories gained 542, and fared badly in a series of by-elections.

A psephologist worked it out that if the performance of swinging London were repeated in a general election the existing Labour majority would be transformed into a Conservative one of 329.

In the inevitable inquests which followed, most people attributed the defeats to the unpopularity of the prices and incomes policy. So long as there was a 'freeze-for-all', the workers had accepted the wages standstill as fair and necessary. But the period of severe restraint seemed to breed inequities and to hold down wages, without effectively controlling prices.

This was certainly Cousins' interpretation. He told a union rally at Poole in Dorset: 'The combination of a wage freeze with continued rents and price increases has spread bewilderment and resentment among many Labour supporters.' He added, however, that it was a mistake for working people not to turn out to vote Labour. In effect, the results of the mini-elections in the spring and early summer of 1967 could be interpreted as a massive non-vote by Labour supporters and trade unionists. They might be said to have voted with their slippers.

Party leaders and officials did not attempt to minimise the seriousness of the setback or to hide their dismay at the massacre of Labour councillors in nearly every city, town and county of Britain. But Ministers, from the Prime Minister downwards, insisted that the Government would not be deflected from its policies. Wilson said:

> To trim national policies to short-run electoral considerations would be a betrayal of our responsibilities to the nation. . . . I believe that, in the end, the British people will recognise that we were right.

He told a May Day rally in Leeds that the Government was now in the second phase of 're-fitting and re-structuring' the national economy and, borrowing from the thoughts of Comrade Mao, declared that we were preparing for the 'great leap forward'. Unfortunately for the Government, most of the economic indicators in the early part of the year seemed to suggest that the British economy was in a state of stagnation, if not on the verge of a 'great leap backwards'. The index of production rose by only $\frac{1}{2}$ per cent in the first quarter, and the May unemployment figure, representing 2·3 per cent of the working population, was the worst May level for four years.

The TUC renewed its pressure on the Government to take off the brakes and found an unexpected ally in Roy Jenkins, the Home Secretary. Jenkins told a London Labour party conference in May that the economic growth was the core of Labour's electoral appeal and that the only way to social progress was 'a rapid rate of growth for the remainder of this Parliament'.

Risking a collision with the TUC and ignoring its election reverses, the Government made it clear that it did not intend to throw the prices and incomes policy overboard. Another White Paper appeared just before Easter, which welcomed the voluntary initiative of employers and unions, but insisted that it was necessary to retain 'reserve powers'. The Prime Minister called these a 'legislative long stop'. Some saw in the White Paper a retreat from the earlier tough attitude of the Department of Economic Affairs and a victory for the 'doves' over the 'hawks'.

There were some concessions, including permission to backdate increases, but the criteria were still fairly stringent. Wage increases, according to this White Paper, could only be justified where they were necessary to enable low-paid workers to maintain a 'reasonable standard of living', or where they were linked to genuine productivity increases. There was still to be a nil norm, with compulsory notification of proposed increases under Part II of the Act, when Part IV lapsed in August. The period during which the Government could delay a price or pay increase was extended from four months to seven months.

The White Paper pleased neither the employers nor the TUC. The employers disliked the idea of permanent price control and said that retrospection would make nonsense of attempts to prevent inflation. George Woodcock called the criteria rigid, unfair and impracticable and said that it would be difficult for the TUC to operate its own voluntary machinery under the shadow of legislation. The TUC, however, accepted the general criteria of productivity agreements and increases to help the lower paid workers. The difficulty immediately emerged: what is a lower paid worker? By and large, the TUC accepted the Cousins figure of £15 a week. It suggested that unions putting in claims of up to £1 a week for workers getting less than £14 a week deserved support.

This was not so cut-and-dried as Cousins' own clear £15 a week national minimum target, but it could be interpreted as a step in that direction.

The Government's policy was embodied in the Prices and Incomes (number 2) Bill, published early in June, which came before the House of Commons for its second reading on June 13th. There were ominous mutterings from the left about the new legislation but, to everybody's amazement, the man who came to the Government's rescue was none other than George Woodcock. He told a meeting of trade union MPs, who had gathered in belligerent mood to protest against this latest threat to trade union freedom, that the new Bill was 'innocuous' and a 'bauble' which would soon die out. It was not so very different, he said, from the Bill which the TUC had accepted in 1965.

Despite Woodcock's contemptuous dismissal of the Bill, no fewer than thirty-two Labour MPs, including Ness Edwards, the Chairman of the trade union group, abstained in the division. The Government secured a majority of only fifty-three, after Michael Stewart had painstakingly plodded through an explanation of why the Government sought another twelve months of powers. The new watchword, said Stewart, would be 'cautious moderation' and the Government would only use its powers sparingly, to back up the voluntary system.

During the summer of 1967 many union conferences came out against the Government's incomes policy and in support of a purely voluntary system. The AEU National Committee, despite the eloquence of Sir William Carron, decided by one vote to reject it.

All these events, in the eyes of most observers of the political scene, added up to the interment of George Brown's prices and incomes policy. They saw as the final nail in the coffin the judgment given by Lord Denning on June 14th, in favour of an appeal by two members of ASSET against the freezing of their pay. *The Times* commented:

> Last year's Prices and Incomes Act has been shown to leak like a sieve. . . . If all trade union leaders had adopted the litigious militancy of Mr Clive Jenkins the policy would now be in shreds.

The Government itself was reconciled to the view that about 12 million workers would be entitled to pay increases during 1967, representing an increase of about 6 per cent for the year.

Many came to bury, not to praise the incomes policy, but some thought the obsequies were premature. The policy, at the least, had secured a valuable breathing-space and the Government still retained vestiges of control. Whatever the final outcome, Government action had galvanised the TUC into establishing its own centralised machinery. The TUC's wage-vetting committee, between November 1966 and July

1967, considered 340 claims covering over 4 million workers, an average of about forty a month.

Frank Cousins was certainly not among those who came to mourn, but neither did he find any joy in being able to say 'I told you so' to his former Ministerial colleagues. As a lifelong Socialist, he did not relish the discomfiture of the Labour Government. The economic problems, coming on top of the international troubles over Vietnam, the Common Market, the Middle East, Rhodesia, Gibraltar and Aden, made the summer of 1967 one of the grimmest periods that this, or any Government, ever had to face. It was, indeed, a summer of discontent.

To cap it, the unemployment figures in August rose to well over half a million, the highest August level for twenty-seven years.

Cousins' public appearances during this period were few and far between—he spent a considerable time abroad on union missions—and, for the first time for many years, he was comparatively neglected in the press. From all accounts, he had been mellowed by time and his unhappy excursion into politics. Some of his unkinder critics said that he was not so much 'mellowed' as 'deflated' or 'subdued'. He had, willy-nilly, become a TUC senior statesman but, here again, there are conflicting reports from eyewitnesses. One of his colleagues said he seemed in a desperate hurry, like a man with only a few months ahead, to put the Government right. Another thought Cousins was taking things relatively easily and only waiting for the moment when he could retire to Cornwall to grow chrysanthemums. A third observer said he seemed to be suffering from a sort of 'Cabinet hangover'. 'He is always pontificating about the balance of payments—as bad as Selwyn Lloyd.'

Cousins' views on the latest phase of the freeze were published in his union journal. He insisted that the TGWU would never have supported the TUC incomes policy, if it meant underwriting Government policy, since the two were mutually incompatible. It would lead to two sets of machinery, operating alongside, with two conflicting sets of delays and conflicting comments and criticisms. He went so far as to threaten non-co-operation:

> The position of our union is clear. We cannot go two ways at once. The dangers of legislative control are so apparent that we would have to say that we would continue to notify the TUC of claims, but we would *not* report to the Government, or heed the decisions of the Prices and Incomes Board.

It did not escape notice that this threat was not so formidable as it sounded, since any claims reported to the TUC would almost certainly eventually find their way to the Prices and Incomes Board.

The Transport and General Workers' Union, under its own steam, went ahead with its campaign for the £15 a week national minimum, with a forty-hour week and three weeks' holiday. This was the theme at every meeting, and in every leaflet and pamphlet issued from Transport House. It was enshrined in the resolution adopted by the Union's conference at Blackpool in July, and two months later was carried by the Trades Union Congress at Brighton.

The 1967 TUC may be held to have marked the vindication of Cousins' policies. It not only unanimously accepted his union's proposals for a £15-a-week minimum, but firmly told the Government to drop all ideas of compulsion. Despite the appeals of Labour loyalists, led by the recently-elevated Peers Carron and Cooper, backed by the ETU President Leslie Cannon, the trade union movement expressed its disenchantment with the Government's economic performance in no uncertain terms. The conference accepted by 4,883,000 votes to 3,502,000 (against the General Council's advice) an omnibus resolution deploring 'the use by the Government of traditional deflationary measures to manage the economy which involve the creation of a pool of unemployed workers', and calling for economic expansion.

Cousins missed the preliminary eve-of-Congress skirmishing on the General Council, when it was decided by eighteen votes to fourteen, to oppose this resolution. He was attending a Labour centenary celebration in Canada and only arrived back on the Tuesday morning. He slipped unobtrusively into his seat with his delegation in the back of the hall, but was immediately pounced on by a battery of press photographers, who gave him the full treatment.

It was in this very same hall, Brighton's Dome, that Cousins had in 1956 begun his long campaign against wage restraint and upset the more orthodox members of the General Council with the violence of his attack on the Government of the day. Eleven years later, he saw his policies accepted without demur and the minority become a majority. For him, the wheel had come full circle.

This time there were no verbal fireworks, but a quiet repetition of the kind of speech he had been making down the years. He emphasised that Britain was not a high wage economy and could well afford a £15 national minimum. Much to the relief of many on the platform, he gave his general blessing to the continuation of the TUC's newly assumed role of an economic general staff.

> If we are going to have a planned and more orderly approach to the idea of fair shares for all, the TUC is the body to give its consideration to the measures we ought to be using.

Cousins was far more moderate in his criticisms of the Government than most other delegates and his speech was as milk and water to Robert Willis's fire and brimstone. Willis, who a few weeks before had resigned from the Prices and Incomes Board, lashed out at the Government:

One has to ask what trust can we any longer place in Government policies, that have rigorously and almost brutally held down wages yet, at the same time, have increased prices and, in the process, presented us with the biggest unemployment problem in postwar years. . . . The Government has had its chance. . . . It had our confidence and trust, and it failed.

He poured scorn on the Prime Minister's decision (announced at the end of August) to assume personal command of economic affairs and to replace Michael Stewart by Peter Shore.

Having known the fiery turbulence of George Brown, having suffered the icy freeze of Michael Stewart, we are now to be led into the mists of indecision by an 'overlord' who is a pastmaster in the art of invective.

Willis spoke more in anger than in sorrow. Cousins, by contrast, seemed to be more sorrowful than angry. 'I think we are entitled to try to guide the Government and this is what this resolution is doing,' he said.

For all George Woodcock had sought to devalue the annual Trades Union Congress as a policy-making body and to dismiss its resolutions as immaterial, Cousins, and indeed the vast majority of the delegates, certainly regarded the decisions of 1967 as a clear statement of union policy which they expected the leadership to implement.

Although Frank Cousins may be regarded as one of the men who did most to upset TUC support for the prices and incomes policy, he has refused to go all the way in condemning the Government. At his own union conference, he deplored suggestions that the TGWU should, as a protest against Government's 'non-socialist' policies, stop paying its affiiliation fees to the Labour party. At a rally at Alexandra Park during the summer, he insisted that the trade unions should continue to support the party. An irreverent London busman in his audience commented:

'If he leans over backwards much further, he'll fall over.'

The pull of conflicting loyalties placed Cousins in a dilemma which has dogged him all his life. First, in his clashes with Gaitskell over the H-bomb and public ownership, and later, as a member of the Cabinet, he had been haunted by the question of just how far he could, and should, go in pressing his opposition to its logical conclusion and using his power to win his way.

He found himself in an even greater dilemma in January 1968 over the municipal busmen's pay claim for £1 a week, which the Minister of Labour had vetoed. No doubt recalling the unhappy experience of the London bus strike, he chose to avoid immediate industrial action and instead to 'do a Clive Jenkins' and take legal action against the employers. The Government retaliated by invoking Part II of the Prices and Incomes Act, freezing the busmen's pay while the issue went before the Prices and Incomes Board. This was the first time that Part II was used to stop a wage increase.

Trade unionists have an ingrained suspicion of law courts, and Cousins was strongly criticised from the right as well as the left. There was also at this time widespread speculation about whether he would continue to support the official TUC incomes policy, when union executives met to consider it. He missed the crucial vote at a meeting, when the General Council accepted the TUC report and his two lieutenants on the Council, deprived of his guidance, abstained. The *Guardian* commented: 'His brinkmanship grows a little more tortuous each day.'

Cousins reacted bitterly to the Government's plans to back up devaluation with cuts in social service spending. 'We are not prepared to have our standard of living cut,' he declared. Equally, he remained determined not to be driven into the arms of the Tories. He had said in October: 'If you get rid of Harold Wilson, the alternative is Ted Heath, and he really is no better than anybody.'

18

Man and motive

W E have now followed Frank Cousins down the years, from the moment he burst so unexpectedly and explosively into the trade union scene in 1956 to the point, eleven years later, when he saw his long fight against wage restraint crowned with success. We have looked at his views on industry and politics, at his relations with his union 'brothers' and his Labour party colleagues, and at his brief experience as a Minister of the Crown and a Member of Parliament. From his own actions and sayings, and from the observations of his contemporaries, some idea of the man's personality has begun to emerge. But he still creates the net impression of a gigantic jigsaw puzzle, and not all the pieces can be fitted in to make a complete whole.

Most people, unless they are at the very top in politics or business, expect to live out their lives on a fairly level plateau, with only intermittent ups and downs. Cousins has experienced violent fluctuations, many of his own creation, moving from peak to trough throughout his career.

The peak of 1956–7, when, as a new broom, he swept all before him at the TUC and at his own union conference, was followed by the trough of 1958, the year of the London bus strike. In 1959–60, he was on top again, and seemed to be swinging the entire movement to his way of thinking on the Bomb. But Hugh Gaitskell successfully hit back.

In 1964, after Labour's election victory, Cousins became a Cabinet Minister and seemed to be at, or near, the pinnacle of power. Twenty months later he resigned. For this, he was vilified by many in the Labour movement and accused of letting down the Government; others applauded his courage in sticking to his principles, at considerable financial sacrifice. Throughout the doldrums of early 1967, when the interminable arguments between the Government and the TUC about prices and incomes seemed to be getting nowhere, Cousins was gradually creeping up. By September, he was on top again.

Whether he will stay there, or whether he will suffer another slump in his fortunes, must be a matter of guesswork. Cousins is due to retire from the leadership of his union in September 1969, when he reaches the age of sixty-five. It is difficult to imagine him in complete retirement, though, after his strenuous career in public life, he might welcome the chance to relax and become a private citizen. There was some speculation in the autumn of 1967 that he might get a job in Barbara Castle's proposed National Freight Authority.

Frank Cousins himself says he is 'simple' and 'straightforward'. Yet to most people he remains something of an enigma. Like all human beings, and rather more than most, Cousins is a mixture of contradictions and complexities. He epitomises the diehard Keir Hardie type of Socialist, with his unquenchable faith in nationalisation and social ownership, and he is also the trade union tycoon, who talks on level terms with the captains of industry. He combines Victorian syndicalism with twentieth century ideas on automation and technology. He is a demagogue, with a charismatic appeal, who can rouse a delegate conference to a pitch of fervour, and he is a cool negotiator, who more than holds his own with employers at the boardroom table. He is a man of simple tastes, who is completely at ease at official functions and receptions. He can be courteous and charming at one moment, and, in a flash of quick temper, become rude and boorish. Uncannily, he manages to be arrogant and diffident, farouche and friendly, at the same time.

To understand the man better, it is necessary to see him against his home background. I have deliberately skated clear of this so far, because a man in public life is entitled to privacy in his home. But his wife Nance has played, and is playing, such an important part in his life, that she cannot be left out of the picture. They are in many ways complementary. They share the same background and the same tastes and interests. Cousins has described how they did their courting at ILP meetings in the early Doncaster days. More recently, they marched hand-in-hand with the nuclear disarmers.

Nance Cousins is to the left of her husband politically and many say she is the better politician. This has sometimes conjured up the vision of a Lady Macbeth, ever at his elbow, stiffening his purpose, holding the dagger poised—and never more so than at the height of the H-Bomb clashes with Gaitskell. Cousins has scoffed at this interpretation. 'What is this talk of influence, when we agree instinctively and whole-heartedly on all major issues?' he once said. Nance Cousins, herself, underrates her influence on her husband. 'Frank makes his own decisions,' she will say. She told a reporter who was badgering her during the London bus strike: 'It has nothing to do with me.' In fact, it had everything to do with her. She lives through her husband's tribulations and triumphs, and is constantly at his side. She will never join the social outings planned by TUC wives at a congress, for fear she might miss a debate where Cousins is speaking.

Anybody who expected to find a sinister *éminence grise* in Nance Cousins would be sadly disillusioned. She is gay, companionable and hospitable, a superb cook and manager, as one would expect from someone who had to bring up a family in the lean thirties. Frank Cousins, incidentally, has never lost the hearty appetite he acquired in his mining days and is appreciative of his wife's cooking.

The Cousinses have four children—and several grandchildren. The eldest son, John, is a former BOAC steward who became an official in his father's union. Michael is a Cambridge-educated scientist, now employed in private industry. The two daughters are Brenda, a housewife, and Frances, whom we met at the opening of this story and who, by 1967, had developed into an extremely attractive miniskirted and self-possessed young woman.

The Cousinses live in Carshalton Beeches, Surrey and, after Cousins' serious heart attack in 1963, bought themselves a cottage near Helston in Cornwall. It is there they spend most of their holidays and there, presumably, that they will settle when Cousins retires, though Nance does not relish the prospect of vegetating in the country.

Cousins is physically a big man, six foot two inches in height, with an erect, almost Guardsman, bearing and steely blue-grey eyes which look at you very straight from behind their large spectacle frame. He has a firm chin and lips which rarely open beyond a half-smile. He lists his recreations in *Who's Who* as 'gardening and reading'. He might have added 'talking politics', for he once said: 'I talk politics everywhere, there isn't much else I talk about.'

Back trouble, brought on by the strain of the London bus strike and a heart attack, put an end to physical exertion, though at one time he enjoyed swimming and dancing, and is still a keen gardener. As the father of a growing family, he kept up to date with jazz and pop music. He does with very little sleep, goes to bed late (as anybody who has joined him socially at a conference will testify) and is an early riser. He enjoys long-distance driving, particularly at night, and is a very good driver. Once a heavy smoker, he gave it up suddenly, showing a strength of purpose which weaker mortals might envy. He had just put a cigarette out during a union meeting, and a colleague pushed over a packet to him. 'No thanks, I've given it up,' he said. He never smoked again.

Cousins, though he has to spend a great deal of time on foreign missions, does not really like 'abroad'. He resents not being able to talk a foreign language for he is never very happy in unfamiliar territory, whether it be Europe or the House of Commons. A friend described him as 'patriotic, almost to the point of insularity'.

This attitude may have contributed, in part, to his 'blow hot, blow cold' view on the Common Market. At the outset he tended to favour Britain's entry into Europe, but he became increasingly cautious and stressed the needs for safeguards for British and Commonwealth interests. He has never shared George Brown's enthusiasm for Europe, and it could be that Brown's advocacy tipped the scales the other way for him. His speech to his own union conference in 1967 was revealing:

> We are not going to have politicians putting a bandage round our eyes and leading us into the Common Market saying 'Trust us'. There have been too many errors of judgment in the past for that.

Most people can be divided into Frankophils and Frankophobes. Very few are completely neutral about him and, from the responses to some of my enquiries, people might have been talking about a totally different man. 'One of the best brains in the country; if he had had a formal education, he could have got any job he wanted,' was the comment of a colleague at the Ministry of Technology, who thought that Cousins would have made a very good chairman and managing director of ICI. Many industrialists and employers' leaders have been loud in their praises, while the attitude of some union officials and members in regions like the Midlands has been little short of sycophantic.

Lord Snow, Parliamentary Secretary to the Ministry of Technology, told a New York audience: 'Cousins is a born intellectual.' Yet many politicians, including some Cabinet Ministers, told me: 'He's a nice man, but stupid.'

'Stupid', perhaps, in that he is politically naive and lacks

o

the finesse or sense of strategy which makes for success in politics. He is, in fact, an intelligent man, without intellectual pretensions, essentially pragmatic in his approach. The *New Statesman*, in a penetrating profile in 1956, said: 'Cousins is no deep abstract thinker; he makes all his deductions from his own experience; he is influenced by what has happened to him.' It observed: 'Frank Cousins believes in Frank Cousins. Seldom can egoism have been more open or more disarming.'

Most of his TUC colleagues regard him as a rather lonely figure, 'prickly' as a cactus, quick to take offence and not a good loser. Yet, however exasperated they may become with him, there are few who do not have a considerable affection for 'Brother' Cousins. Many react subjectively according to the way he has treated them. Journalists have often been at the receiving end of his impatience, and it is worth recalling a few incidents which reveal his attitude towards the press.

In 1956 I had written a profile for the *News Chronicle*, to coincide with the announcement of his election as General Secretary of the Transport Union. As the result was a foregone conclusion, my paper decided to publish it on the morning the announcement was due and I inadvertently, and ill-advisedly, mentioned this to Cousins. He was furious that a newspaper should seek to jump the gun, and that evening rang up the night desk and persuaded them to leave it out. Only the readers in the far north of Scotland or south-west England who received the first edition were able to read my prophetic opening words: 'The name Frank Cousins may not be very well known to the general public, but it soon will be.'

The incident is not important, but it illustrates Cousins' own character, as well as the spinelessness of the *News Chronicle*. One can hardly imagine Arthur Christiansen of the *Express*, or Hugh 'Publish and be damned' Cudlipp of the *Daily Mirror* changing their paper's make-up at the behest of a trade union leader, however powerful.

Towards the end of the London bus strike, when a settlement was about to be reached, Len Jackson, the man from the *Mirror*, politely suggested that the news would reach union members more quickly if the papers were allowed to publish the details, rather than wait for the official circular. Cousins glared at him. 'We don't run our union for the benefit of Fleet Street,' he said icily.

When he was Minister of Technology he was asked to give a TV interview at London Airport on his return from a visit to the USA. He was warned that it might have to be cut. 'Cut?' said Frank. 'Not me, you don't.'

It is not surprising that Cousins should be wary about the press, in view of the treatment he received at various crisis-points in his career. He has not forgotten the way in which one paper snooped into his hotel bill at Oxford, nor the pursuit by some reporters of young Frances when she was still at school, or of Michael, when he was working at the atomic energy plant at Windscale. He shares, to an exaggerated extent, the instinctive suspicion of many Labour leaders about the capitalist press, although he is extremely good friends with individual industrial correspondents.

Cousins long resisted the idea that it might be an advantage for the Union to have a public relations department. 'We're not selling soap, you know,' he told a union conference where the proposal was being debated. His 'image' both as union leader and Minister might have been better if he had paid more attention to modern techniques of public relations. He has, however, achieved a great deal of success as a performer on television and radio, where the qualities of sincerity and conviction really count.

Cousins delivers his public speeches at a machine-gun speed, and his cascade of words often gives the impression that he is thinking on his feet. Sometimes his meaning is ambiguous and his syntax confused, but he avoids the circumlocution and clichés which so often adorn trade union speeches. (Ernie Bevin once said of a colleague that his speeches were 'as full of "clichés" as a hospital is of bed-pans'.) Cousins does, in fact, prepare his speeches fairly carefully.

He is, as we have noted, at his happiest and most at ease among his union rank and file, his own 'people', at conferences and socials, or over a friendly drink. There is something almost paternal in his make-up, though it never reaches the point of being patronising. This is particularly noticeable when he is dealing with people in a relationship of comradely authority, as in his own union or in the Nuneaton Labour party. Unlike some left-wing MPs of my acquaintance, who tend to vent their spleen on waiters, Cousins is courtesy itself to those who have to earn their living by serving others. If he had a valet he would doubtless be a hero to him.

To his friends and admirers Cousins is a crusader, carrying high the banner of true Socialism. To some he is a Don Quixote, tilting at windmills, while his opponents have often regarded him as a Frankenstein monster and Maverick. Woodrow Wyatt described him in 1960 as 'a bully, rampaging round like a rogue elephant, arrogant, ambitious and suicidal in his efforts to sabotage the Labour party'. (It is fair to say that by 1966, Woodrow Wyatt was sharing some of Cousins' views on economic policy and defence.)

Even among his fiercest critics, I have never heard anybody question his sincerity. 'Completely honest' was the verdict of a big union leader who differed violently from his politics. Cousins himself made this cryptic but revealing remark at the *Tribune* rally at Brighton in October 1966: 'A man's reputation is no bigger than his integrity.' Integrity is a quality he takes pride in himself and looks for in others. He once said: 'I like children very much. They are perfectly honest, and there are not many people that one can say that about.'

Nor has it ever been suggested that he is financially ambitious. On the contrary, he often expressed embarrassment that he should be receiving a fat Ministerial salary at a time when the Government was seeking to impose restraint on the lower-paid workers. His return to his union meant a big drop in salary. Even though his general secretary's salary of £3,750 a year is high by British trade union standards, it would make any American union leader blench. James Hoffa, of the Teamsters' Union, was said to command the equivalent of £35,700 a year.

What has been the main driving-force in his career as a union leader? It has certainly not been money, or social prestige. A union official (one of the few who consistently stood up to him) said that Cousins was impelled by a lust for power and that his decision to leave the Government meant that he had contracted out of 'the power game'.

This is an over-simplification. Cousins certainly wants to exercise power, but it is a power which derives from the Union and which he seeks to use for the Union. He made a revealing admission at a TGWU rally in 1964, soon after he had joined the Government, and could therefore be presumed to have reached the top flight of power:

> The greatest power that any man has is in his union. When I talk outside, they don't listen to my voice alone, they listen to the voices of 1,500,000 members, they listen everywhere, everywhere.

By this token, it might be said that if Cousins' voice did not represent 1½ million votes it would not command the same universal attention. Were he the leader of a small union, he might be listened to with respect, as an intelligent man with strong convictions, but he would not wield much power.

Possibly the most compelling motive in his union life has been his hostility (hatred might be too strong a word) for Arthur Deakin, which contrasted sharply with his admiration for Bevin, whom he once described as 'the greatest trade union leader we have had up to now'. 'Never compare me with Deakin. Some day I hope to merit comparison with Bevin,' he once confided to a friend. He regarded Deakin's authoritarianism as incompatible with his own concept of social democracy, in which a new order would be based on the workers' genuine participation.

Bevin could be brutal, as Ben Tillett discovered in the 1920s when he was stripped of his place and power in the Union. George Lansbury felt it, too, when, at Brighton in 1935, Bevin accused him of 'trailing his conscience round from body to body asking to be told what to do with it'. Cousins was more soft-hearted and less vindictive, and some of his left-wing supporters have said that a touch of the Tillett/Lansbury treatment for some of his more elderly right-wing officials would have been salutary.

Cousins may have lacked the ruthless streak, as well as the rocklike strength, of Ernest Bevin, but he shared many of his qualities and defects. Essentially English, pragmatic and single-minded, they had a common faith in the workers and identified themselves completely with their union. Bevin, like Cousins, could be arrogant and prickly, and resented the criticism which is the lot of any man in public life.

Not all his supporters thought that Cousins went far enough in the process of 'De-deakinisation' of the TGWU. Jack Dash, the unofficial dockers' leader, said: 'I think he is the finest General Secretary I have ever met,' but some of the militant London busmen accused him of not being sufficiently 'political', or putting his ideas into practice. One of them complained to me in the winter of 1966 that Cousins had failed to carry his fight against the prices and incomes policy to its logical conclusion, by enlisting the Union's massive industrial power to compel a change.

'He's all bark and no bite—he talks like Jesus Christ, but he acts like Arthur Deakin,' he said. 'The man's a paper tiger.'

Why, in the event, did Cousins not use the Union's power

to compel a change in the policy upon which he felt so strongly as to resign? To extremists, like my London busman, it was a sign of cowardice. To his right-wing critics, he was the bomb that didn't go off, the 'ineffectual angel', as Matthew Arnold said of Shelley. Both versions are wide of the mark. In fact, Cousins' attitude since his resignation fits into the general pattern of his behaviour throughout his career.

He has always insisted on using constitutional and democratic methods, rather than force, to get his way. If his members, in any section—whether bus, British Oxygen or car delivery—were prepared to press their claims to the point of withdrawing their labour, he would back them. If they were not, he would not. It was as simple as that.

Shortly before Christmas, the Cabinet was discussing the incomes policy. 'We owe Frank Cousins a vote of thanks,' said one member. 'He had it in his power to wreck the national economy, but he did not use it.' It is doubtful whether Cousins would have appreciated a vote of thanks from a Cabinet, which so 'irritated' him and from which he had so recently resigned. But he could certainly be gratified that, as we saw in the last chapter, opinion in the trade union movement had come round, without precipitating industrial conflict, to the viewpoint which he had so persistently advocated.

The relations between Cousins and George Woodcock have sometimes been compared with those between Bevin and Citrine, who held parallel roles as leader of the country's biggest trade union and General Secretary of the TUC. Although the relations between Bevin and Citrine were often acrimonious, and Bevin harboured suspicions about Citrine's motives, the two men shared the same global approach to trade union problems and both contributed to the formation of the modern trade union movement. Nearly thirty years later the co-operation between the General Secretaries of the

TUC and the TGWU, based on far better personal relationships, helped to produce a working formula for the development of the TUC as it approached its centenary.

A strong and efficient trade union movement is essential to the health of Britain, and the decision by individual unions to vest greater authority in the TUC marked an important step towards this aim. Without Cousins' approval of this development, as was shown in Chapter 16, it is doubtful whether such a decision would have been taken. History is still in the making, and it is impossible to forecast the effect of the new trend within the TUC. While cynics say that the unions will slip back into their old anarchy as soon as George Woodcock has retired, others believe that the foundations laid in 1966 will prove lasting.

It is also impossible, and would be unfair, to attempt any final assessment of Cousins' leadership of the Transport and General Workers' Union. Future historians will certainly not rate him on a par with Bevin, who surely ranks as one of Britain's great labour leaders. But Cousins' departure from the trade union stage, on which he has played such a leading and controversial part, will leave a very large gap. Men of principle are not all that common in British public life.

Bibliography

THE LIFE AND TIMES OF ERNEST BEVIN, Vol. I. Alan Bullock, Heinemann, Vol. I 1960, Vol. II 1967.

ERNEST BEVIN, Francis Williams, Hutchinson, 1952.

BEVIN, Trevor Evans, Allen & Unwin, 1946.

TRADE UNION LEADERSHIP, V. L. Allen, Longmans Green & Co., 1957.

THE GOVERNMENT OF BRITISH TRADE UNIONS, J. Goldstein, Allen & Unwin, 1952.

THE BRITISH GENERAL ELECTION OF 1964 and THE BRITISH GENERAL ELECTION OF 1966, D. E. Butler & A. King, Macmillan, 1965 and 1966.

IN PLACE OF FEAR, A. Bevan, Heinemann, 1952.

HUGH GAITSKELL, W. T. Rodgers, Thames & Hudson, 1964.

THE FAWLEY PRODUCTIVITY AGREEMENT, A. Flanders, Faber, 1964.

WHAT IS WRONG WITH TRADE UNIONS, E. Wigham, Penguin Special, 1960.

TRADE UNIONS AND THE LABOUR PARTY, M. Harrison, Allen & Unwin, 1960.

LIFE OF STAFFORD CRIPPS, Colin Cooke, 1957.

THE DISARMERS, Christopher Driver, Hodder & Stoughton, 1964.

FAITH UNDER FIRE, Canon J. L. Collins, Frewin, 1965.

Annual reports and publications of the Trades Union Congress.

Annual reports and publications of the Labour Party.

The *Record*, Journal of the Transport and General Workers' Union.

TGWU minutes of evidence to Royal Commission on Trade Unions and Employers Associations, HMSO, 1966.

TUC evidence to Royal Commission, TUC, 1966.

Ministry of Labour Gazette.

Hansard, House of Commons official reports.

Index